Barter Your Way

to Greater Wealth

By:

Robert Borneman

This Work is Dedicated to

My Ever Loving Wife Joy,

My Trading Partner!

IT'S TIME
TO TRADE IN
YOUR OLD WAY OF
DOING BUSINESS,
FOR A NEW ONE

TABLE OF CONTENTS

PROLOGUE

Barter is about improving your bottom line, making larger profits, improving your balance sheet and acquiring new assets with lower costs than other businesses or your competition. Bartering will also allow you to improve your personal lifestyle, whether that is accomplished through the bottom line growth of a business you own or simply by trading on a personal level.

I will give you some insight about why you should be bartering and more importantly, HOW you should be bartering. I've broken the process down step by step with the intent of inspiring and motivating you to start trading now, and I will explain the math behind the science of bartering. Many new and unusual opportunities will come your way when you enter the world of barter; this book will help you be prepared to take advantage of the ones that are right for you.

In the early nineties, I was working in one of my jewelry stores when Mike, a customer who owned a tree trimming business, told me about a barter exchange he belonged to and convinced me to join. Looking back over a highly successful lifetime, I would say it was definitely one of the top five positive decisions I've made in the last thirty something years that propelled my business forward. As it turns out, Mike approached me at a most opportune time.

My business was struggling with high debt and weak cash flow, meaning there was hardly enough money coming in to pay the existing bills, and new ones were coming in every day. Bartering was one of the primary tools I used to improve my cash flow and reduce my debt, while at the same time increasing my sales volume. Bartering improved my ability to advertise, make new customers and deal directly with other business owners, saving me lots of cash. I had a large amount of success trading and in 1996, *Newsday,* a Long Island newspaper, ran a story on barter telling a little bit of my story. The complete article can be found just before the appendix.

While my story may not be the greatest success story of all time, it is nonetheless a story of rags to riches beyond normal expectations fueled in part by bartering. I started my business in 1978, just three years after high school, with a forty dollar loan from my Mom to buy a costume jewelry kit that consisted of a dozen rings and a small catalog that we wrote orders from.

Thanks to the help from my Mom, Brothers, Sister and my Girlfriend who is now my Wife, we grew the jewelry business from working out of a briefcase into a highly successful fine jewelry business generating several million dollars per year in sales that spun off other business opportunities in the real estate, motion picture and restaurant industries. Now I'm part of the *"one percenter's",* earning an income the media implies is too much, but I'm okay with it, and you will be too, as you earn your way there.

I think my first barter transaction was about two hundred dollars for a ring I sold to Mike which paved the way to *trading* for several million dollars' worth of goods and services since then, in addition to my cash business.

My wife and I still own and operate Diamond Jewelers, on Long Island in New York, the centerpiece of our business investments and our family is still working with us. We still barter regularly and use our trade dollars and extra cash flow to buy everything from business supplies to vacations. Often in this book when I refer to "my" company or say "I", that really means "our" company and "we" because my true secret to success has been surrounding myself with my family and others who have expertise in areas I do not; and so together we have been able to grow our business in ways I could never have done alone.

This writing, like so many of the wonderful things that have occurred in my life, would not have been possible without the continuous oversight and support from my loving wife Joy. I would also like to thank my sister in-law Louise and friends Ken and Linda for their support and assistance with editing this project. I am forever deeply indebted to my mom Gloria,

my brother Jim and Sister Diane for much of my success, and

dedicate this work to them as well.

BARTER IS ABOUT CREATING RELATIONSHIPS

CHAPTER 1

WHY YOU SHOULD BARTER

Since I started bartering, I have traded a few million dollars of jewelry for everything from the ordinary to the outlandish and that sum is peanuts compared to companies that barter more than this in one year. I have purchased items for my business; including advertising, art, jewelry, business supplies, auto repairs for company vehicles, legal and professional services and even merchandise that I have resold for cash. I have also purchased personal items including: real estate, vacations, jewelry, art, apparel, electronics and basic services like dry cleaning, auto repair, home maintenance and dentistry, plus so much more.

Throughout this book, I will provide you with detailed tips for making intelligent choices and decisions that will enhance your ability to become successful at bartering.

Hopefully you noticed I said jewelry and art twice in my opening paragraph, this was not a typo because some of these items can be a personal expense or a business expense. How you use and ultimately classify what you buy determines if an item is tax deductible and we will explore this difference as it relates specifically to barter transactions in great detail later on.

You might also have noticed I put real estate in the business category, which I did because I purchased a home that could have been used as a personal residence, but I used it as an income producing asset. By renting it and classifying it as a business asset, since I also have a real estate business, I am able to deduct expenses for maintenance and depreciate the cost of the property over time. Had I elected to live in the house I bartered for, it would have been a personal expense and most of the expenses associated with maintaining it would not be tax deductible.

Asset Conversion

Barter is not just about the traditional mindset of swapping or trading merchants' wares, it is about turning unproductive assets into more useful assets.

These assets include your time, your staffs' time, your inventory, unused or unwanted office equipment, furniture or supplies, antiquated or idle manufacturing equipment, personal property or anything not serving its intended purpose that is now collecting dust that can be traded for something you can use. You will also learn that it can be much easier to trade many of these things for greater than their inherent cash value than it is to sell them.

Unlimited Benefits

How can you benefit the most from bartering? The answer usually lies within how you value time and money, your primary assets in business and life. *Time and Money*, two of the most precious and sought after things most of us would like to have more of, yet we usually have much more of one than the other to work with. If you have time available and could use more money, then barter is definitely going to benefit you and/or your business.

Why should you barter? Simply stated; to make more money and accumulate more assets! Whether you are a newcomer hoping to learn about how to delve into the world of barter or an experienced trader looking to pick up some tips to advance your bartering skills, I would like to share some secrets with you. I'll even share the dirty secrets of trading that I have discovered. I would also like to let you know about some tips that you can benefit from immediately and important pitfalls to avoid. All in all, the ideas in this book encompass much of my thirty five years of bartering experiences that I hope will set you on a path leading you to greater financial strength and personal wealth.

Cash Flow

Cash flow is the life blood of a business. Cash flow is not your income, it's the money you have on hand, constantly moving in and out of your business to pay your expenses and hopefully draw income against. Having the ability to improve your cash flow exponentially without even creating new sales is a powerful benefit of bartering! When combined with creating new sources of cash flow this becomes one of the primary reasons you should be bartering. Whether you are an entrepreneur starting out or a seasoned business person, the value extra cash flow creates in managing your business cannot be understated. It relieves financial pressure and mental stress allowing managers to manage their businesses and focus on growth. Recognizing opportunities to create new sources of cash flow are essential to maximizing your barter experience. Therefore, there are many segments throughout this book that outline specific ways to enhance your cash flow.

Fill Your Appointment Book

If you are running a business with time on your hands or your paid employees are waiting around for the phone to ring with the next service call, then make appointments with barter clients to reduce down time in a manner that benefits you.

Are you a carpet cleaner, chimney sweeper or housekeeper with availability on your calendar? Then you should be maximizing this time to accumulate trade dollars that you can use to make your business run smoother. Yes, the butcher, the baker and the candlestick maker should be bartering! You will find there is a direct correlation between how much you increase your profitability through barter and how much more enjoyable it is to run your business. Use barter to find new clients that can fill these gaps in your schedules and create new revenue for yourself.

Improve Your Image in Town

As you establish trade relationships and start reducing or eliminating basic expenses that drain your cash like advertising, printing and so forth, you can begin to focus on ways to improve your business and make new investments that will bring more cash your way. A great way to increase your exposure in the community is to put out new signs, update the ones you have, hang some banners, improve your landscaping, repaint or add siding to an aging building and increase the curb appeal of your business. All of these things will be noticed by the people who shop in your area and should encourage more people to visit your place of business while elevating your image in the community.

Liquidate Inventory

Stale inventory, sometimes an unavoidable and necessary evil, is the nemesis of turnover in a retail environment. Stale inventory raises carrying costs and reduces growth because of aging, low turnover or seasonality, which is why most retailers mark merchandise down. Sometimes markdowns occur to make room for new arrivals.

From now on, don't mark anything down, trade it to maximize the dollars you have invested in items that just don't sell.

Expend less handling time, free up useful display space that should be earning you money and put new products out that will sell. Barter the stale items, reduce redundancy in your stock and go on vacation, do something extravagant or bank a few dollars with the extra money.

Marketing

Marketing is an inherent benefit of bartering in the passive and proactive sense. In its proactive form; trading for signs, banners, flyers, radio spots, TV commercials, billboards, print advertising, promotional products, web design, graphic design and more will launch or supplement your current marketing efforts. In its passive form, bartering brings new customers who create referrals and promote for you. The power that word of mouth exposure has will improve your business by creating extra traffic and new clients which can never be fully evaluated, but will certainly result in added value. The additional traffic you will enjoy also sends a subliminal message to others who visit you. A busier environment often stimulates more sales and well-coordinated efforts can create buying frenzies, generating even more interest in your business. Every new customer represents an opportunity to create another ambassador of good will for you. Always be aware of, and continuously search for, new growth opportunities you can create through your developing base of barter customers, which is a renewable resource.

Cross Promotions

Barter with the florists, spas and upscale restaurants in your area for gift certificates and give them to customers with a purchase to stimulate sales on a particular item, category or service in your business.

Use barter to gain an edge over your competitors and make your business the one in town that's fun to visit.

Swap gift certificates with businesses that compliment yours and share customers with other businesses that are willing to promote your business. You can do this with coupons as well as gift certificates where you're offering a discount rather than a free service. A gift certificate doesn't have to have a dollar denomination; it could be for a gift with a purchase or a specific service such as a free pedicure. When a customer redeems a certificate you bartered, you have just created a chance to make a new customer and convert trade dollars into new cash flow. Spend some time developing offers that are creative to improve results that meet your goals. Also be sure to spend time with these new customers and make an extra effort to cultivate these relationships so they do come back and spend money with you!

Talent

There are a lot of very talented people out there. Are you one of them? Do you have a special gift or expertise? Maybe you're a musician, an artist, a designer or a home baker with a talent that you would like to share with others. Are you a leader in your field or a consultant that others could benefit from your experience and knowledge? The more you think about new ways to market yourself through barter, the more opportunities you will create that will lead to better exposure and ultimately the ability to earn more cash using your talent.

There's certainly no reason to have a hidden talent, let the rest of us know what you can do!

New Customers

Boots on the ground, that's what every business needs, people marching in your door with wants and needs for you to fill. Traditional advertising is an expensive way to find new business, but you could be trading something you sell or do for the opportunity to grow your customer base. If you're in the type of business that customers frequent such as a bagel shop or bakery, then the value you will receive from trading extra baked goods that may often be disposed of for advertising increases exponentially as every new customer you obtain can be worth significantly more than your initial investment to find them. If your goal is to find new customers, then barter to do so in ways you could not have afforded to before. Build your presence on the web, start a fresh marketing campaign, hit the airwaves or tell your story in magazines; all of these can be traded for and will bring new boots or maybe sandals, to your doorstep.

Customers Are Customers

There should be no discrimination when bartering, customers are customers and just because they are spending trade dollars instead of cash, this doesn't mean they should be treated any differently than your cash customers.

Don't change your business ethics or practices, or let your staff make distinctions in the services you provide when you trade with others, as treating everyone you do business with the same way will pay dividends for years to come. You may have certain guidelines or limitations on the types of transactions you are able to make, but your barter customers are not second class citizens. In fact, you will quickly realize that these new customers are professionals and other business owners in your community you now have a rare one-on-one opportunity to talk with and learn from, in an environment that would not otherwise exist.

Your new found customers and friends will go out of their way to refer cash paying customers when treated properly.

Why else would you know all five dentists in your town, when normally you might only see one regularly? I've learned a lot about other businesses from people I bartered with and found new ways to improve my own business. From conversations with other professionals I've also gleaned new sources to create business and ways to save money that had not previously occurred to me. I get recommendations for places to shop or eat and have made friends that I still socialize with decades after our first barter transaction. As if that were not enough, barter customers may spend money improving your cash business and provide sources for future cash business through referrals.

Be Goal Oriented

Setting goals will help you make better barter transactions and have a more satisfying trading experience. Know what you want and work towards meeting your needs. Are you seeking new customers, more exposure, additional income or cash flow relief? These are all related concepts but you can focus on any of them. Are you looking to grow your sales or introduce a new product to a market place with little promotional costs? Do you want to expand your business or downsize and clear out inventory and fixtures? Do you want to attain higher profit margins or exploit any of the benefits outlined here to maximize your experience in the world of trading? Bartering is a much more sophisticated way of doing business than many people believe. Create a plan and stick to it so you can realize your goals. There is nothing like having a benchmark to compare progress against and measure your success.

Something Odd Might Happen

Bartering can be the catalyst that grows your business, sending new customers your way and increasing your sales to a point where you not only become less financially dependent on bartering to grow your business, but find you have less time to pursue it because you are so much busier generating hard cash. If you excel at trading it can become something akin to a self-fulfilling prophecy in the sense that you start out bartering to improve your cash business and you become busier so you have less time to barter. It happens to us every now and then when we are so busy selling for cash that we don't have the time to spend our trade dollars. Over the years our commitment to bartering has ebbed and flowed. This is not to say that we stop trading, I couldn't imagine that day coming, but our trading activity does slow significantly at times. Some years we have healthy cash flow when our cash business strengthens and we rely less on trade than we do in other years when we become very aggressive at trading.

CREATE NEW REVENUE
AND MAKE
NEW FRIENDS

CHAPTER 2

INTRODUCTION TO BARTER

Long before paper money was created, merchants traded with their customers for goods and services; then the *art of trading* gave way to exchanging currency for goods and services to facilitate transactions. I say the art of trading because although a currency may have an established value, when trading there often are no specific standards, rules or methods of valuation. Whatever you swap, regardless of its value to you, it may be valued quite differently by your trading partner. Ideally each trader will feel they have received a good value or derived a significant benefit from every barter transaction.

Recently, bartering is being rediscovered and utilized by many savvy business people. Economic downturns, such as our most recent prolonged one, play a large role in the volume or ebb and flow of barter transactions that occur. As cash tightens we naturally seek other ways to acquire the things we want or need, and barter is another path to acquire them. Barter or Trade as it is commonly referred to, can be the road to financial freedom or the tool that increases your sales growth exponentially and increases your personal wealth in difficult times, and in prosperous times as well.

Bartering can create positive cash flow, provide tax relief, bring new cash business to your door and barter can be the salvation for many troubled businesses in difficult economic times, as it was for me. There is so much more to be said about why you should barter and *"Barter Your Way to Greater Wealth"*, that I have decided to put this book together to share a *new* way of doing business with you, that actually dates back to the very first business transaction.

I'm sure you have heard of the concept of barter, and maybe you have completed a barter transaction before, but like everything else in life, being the best, or better than most, at something you do gives you an advantage, an edge, which in this case means a way to increase your gross revenues and create greater personal wealth.

As a small business owner, operating several fine jewelry stores over the years, I have constantly been contacted by people looking to sell me something that they believe I *definitely* need or something that they believe will *definitely* increase my sales, but it always comes with a price. Obviously there are never any real guarantees that what they suggest is the answer to one's success; they are sales pitches. If you've been in business for more than a day, you probably know exactly what I mean.

When I said they wanted my hard earned money, I meant it; I started my business with forty dollars I borrowed from my Mom. From this humble beginning, working out of a briefcase, we built our network of jewelry stores and real estate ventures working all day, every day, for the first few years and plowing every penny back into the business. I was able to do this because I was in my early twenties, had very little overhead and I still lived at home with Mom.

I've developed an interesting dichotomy in my business life that my wife always points out to me every time we go to buy something, even if it's for our home. I love to sell, but hate to be sold. Like most of us, I fear being sold something I don't want or need by a salesperson and hate when someone tries to talk me into buying something they "know I need" or is "guaranteed to improve my business".

What an odd paradox for a person who sells jewelry you might think. It actually reinforced my personal values and beliefs which translate to how I interact with my customers and why I have a brutal sense of honesty and assumption of responsibility for anything that goes wrong, regardless of what that can cost me. At times I have paid handsomely for my mistakes, but I not only learned from those experiences, I have become better from them.

So why did I tell you this? To explain how I came to learn about barter. I was having an idle conversation with a customer of mine one day while he was waiting for my jeweler to complete his repair. He was a regular customer who owned a tree trimming business, and we had spoken several times about our respective businesses during his previous visits to my store. One of my primary interests in business is marketing so I always take the opportunity to talk with other entrepreneurs that have the time and inclination to share ideas with me.

The conversation we were having centered on things we were trying to do to improve our respective businesses. During this discussion he asked me if I had ever tried bartering as he had just recently done so himself. He also said that it had helped him out quite a bit, so I inquired how; and listened rather intently as I wondered why I hadn't heard this from someone else before. By the end of the conversation, I asked him if he could give me a contact to explore this further, and so it began.

Now, more than thirty years later, I have come full circle and bring to you what I have experienced and learned. In addition to my thoughts, ideas and the fruits of trial and error in my business endeavors, I have assembled an appendix with sources of additional information and some contacts for you to avail yourself of when bartering.

The Basics

To start with the basics, we will define barter as an exchange of products or services with a buy and sell side to them. What you "give" in the transaction is considered a sale and what you "receive" is considered a buy. When I say *buy* or *sell*, you can substitute the word *trade* because no cash actually changes hands like a traditional sale. Your accountant will still classify each transaction as revenue or an expense on your books, which will be called credits and debits in accounting language. I will work mostly with layman's terms to avoid confusion.

Let's say you sell vacuums, and I own a jewelry store. The simplest form of a barter transaction would be a *Direct Trade* where you *sell* me a vacuum cleaner valued at three hundred dollars retail and I give you a piece of jewelry valued at three hundred dollars retail. In this transaction we do not exchange money or owe each other anything and we are even. As discussed later in detail, if you live in a state where sales tax is collected on the sale of a vacuum cleaner or jewelry, then there would be a sales tax liability which is addressed under the sub heading of *Sales Taxes* in the chapter titled *Taxes*. You would also want to have a system in place to account for this transaction for income tax purposes. Accounting for barter transactions is discussed in the *Taxes* chapter also.

Unlike the thought process of buying something for cash; which is really a trade or an exchange that is not traditionally analyzed as I'll *trade my cash* for a new pair of slacks by consumers; bartering should be thought of as a two sided transaction. The reasons for this will become clearer when we discuss the valuations of trade dollars later. In this transaction, you as the seller of the vacuum cleaner also become the buyer of the jewelry and I as the seller of the jewelry become the buyer of the vacuum cleaner. Both of us actually represent the buyer and seller side of a simple transaction. Even though this sounds very basic, we need to start retraining ourselves to think about how we benefit from each side of a transaction separately.

The next form of a barter transaction would be one involving three parties. Now suppose I called you to tell you how happy I was with the vacuum you sold me and wanted to know if I could get three more for my other stores plus one for my home for a total of twelve hundred dollars. You might be willing to trade for another piece of jewelry or you might not. The tables might even turn when you come into my store and find a five thousand dollar piece of jewelry you like, but I couldn't use enough vacuums to make up the difference. If neither of us have extra cash to balance the value in the deal we could not make the transaction work. How might you resolve this dilemma so both parties can benefit? The answer is by using a *Trade Exchange*.

Trade Exchanges

A Trade Exchange is a clearing house for barter transactions. Trade exchanges replace the need for cash currency to consummate a deal. As a third party, acting as a representative for the buyer and seller, a trade exchange essentially substitutes its own currency for cash. Trade exchanges also provide many services which are described throughout these pages.

A trade exchange is an organization comprised of members who are business owners and professionals with products and services to offer. Anything that can be bought or sold by a member for cash can be traded through a trade exchange for barter credits. A barter credit or trade dollar is assumed to be equal to a cash dollar and is recognized as equal in value by the IRS for tax and accounting purposes. However, you will learn as you read on that there are very distinct differences in how you can accumulate barter or trade dollars to increase

your cash flow and profitability. Contrary to popular belief,

trade dollars or credits are not necessarily less valuable than

cash; in fact the opposite is true quite often.

You will learn that trade dollars do not have the same purchasing power as cash, hence the importance of understanding how to leverage your trade dollars to make them more powerful than cash, making bartering work to your advantage.

In the simplest terms, here's what would happen in a

transaction like the one described above where you as the

vacuum salesman wanted the five thousand dollar ring and I

wanted the four vacuums for twelve hundred dollars. You

would sell me the four vacuums and receive a twelve hundred

dollar credit in your trade exchange account and I would sell

you the ring and get a five thousand dollar credit in my

exchange account. The exchange would then charge your

account the five thousand dollars for the ring you bought and

you would owe the exchange thirty eight hundred barter

dollars instead of owing it to me, representing the difference

of the price of the ring and the vacuums.

On the opposite side of the transaction, I would have a credit for the ring of five thousand dollars less the twelve hundred dollars for the vacuums so I would have a positive balance of thirty eight hundred dollars in my account. Since I don't need any more vacuums, I will use the balance in my account to buy something I need or want from another merchant who is a member of the exchange. I made a nice sale that I probably would not have made to you for cash, so I just created a new revenue source through barter by selling the ring. You have just traded your inventory for a ring you may not have otherwise considered buying for cash. This example is a two way trade using the exchange as a clearing house to account for a difference in the values of the items being traded.

Exchanges facilitate trades in another way you could call *one way* trades. These occur when the parties do not buy and sell from each other as a swap; instead you come into my store and buy jewelry in return for trade credits. This eliminates the need of having to sell me your product or service to make a deal. This form of transaction allows me to trade with many more members too. I accept the exchanges currency in lieu of cash or a swap of products and bank my credits with the trade exchange so I can use them for whatever I desire in the future. This allows me to sell in a barter transaction *without* having to buy or vice versa for you.

Now I have the thirty eight hundred dollars in my account, so I visit a local restaurant and spend ninety dollars on dinner. I don't give the restaurateur any money; instead I sign a barter slip. This works the same way as a credit card charge slip except the trade exchange handles the transaction. Just like a credit card processing bank, the exchange allows me to *charge* my purchase and I get a reduction from my thirty eight hundred dollar balance on my statement at the end of the month. The statement will also show I spent ninety dollars and my balance is now adjusted accordingly to three thousand seven hundred and ten dollars.

In this manner, I can *spend down* some of my account balance at the restaurant while conserving my cash. Using an exchange this way allows *fractional trading* of the original five thousand dollar sale with many trading partners because of the accounting systems provided by trade exchanges.

This doesn't usually happen in a direct trade environment because the accounting becomes too cumbersome for most individuals. It might work with a handful of trading partners but it won't work so well with a hundred or a few thousand traders. For these volumes of trading the bookkeeping would be a huge job and is why exchanges are so important. The nature of these types of transaction has created a need for exchanges and keeps them in business. Basically the ability to bring so many members together to make trades allows exchanges to make money as a matchmaker.

How Much Barter Should You Do?

There is no definitive formula to use, but you should be guided by the size of your inventory or the amount of spare time you can afford to invest and the amount of value you find when spending your trade dollars. If you have little to no costs to sell products or provide services then you could accumulate unlimited trade dollars and benefit tremendously from bartering.

I would estimate that bartering accounts for about ten to fifteen percent of my total business sales on an annual basis, which is a comfortable amount for me. My trading volume does rise and fall based on many factors such as my retail business cycle, the amount of cash I have on hand, the deals that come across my desk and the time I have to pursue deals. All of these factors weigh in on my ability to barter even more effectively, bringing an old adage to mind; there is always room for improvement. Using a trade exchange and a broker to work on my behalf creates opportunities for me accomplish more! While these are only a few reasons affecting how much you should barter, the amount of cash savings or income you develop over time should ultimately be the deciding factor.

Another significant consideration that should affect the amount of trading you do will be whether you are lowering or increasing your tax liability when you barter.

The rule of thumb is simple, the more you spend down your trade dollars for legitimate tax deductible business expenses, the lower your tax burden will be and the more you spend on non-deductible personal expenses, the higher your tax burden will be.

This assumes of course that all other aspects of your tax liabilities remain the same. Spending more on personal items is not a negative; in fact, I would argue it's a positive because you are improving your lifestyle. Paying more taxes can be palatable if you derive benefits to justify the expense. Remember, just because you have generated extra income and spent it on personal items doesn't mean you will have to pay more taxes. You may have other expenses or accrued deductions that offset this income when you file your tax return.

How You Benefit

If you are running a company and you have staff, then you can maximize the value and use of their time by bartering goods or services to increase your overall productivity while managing your assets much more efficiently. Idle staff is what I consider a hidden asset because the payroll is a sunk cost in most cases. Assuming you cannot reduce staffing levels any further; managers are usually tasked with or challenged by how to improve the productivity of idle hands.

Barter provides a solution that can unlock the value in this hidden and often overlooked asset of idle time.

If you are a professional selling your expertise and experience, or you are in a service business without employees where you *are* the business, then the value of your time needs to be maximized. Aside from hiring and training others to do what you do, there is another way to grow your business and thereby earn more income. If you have free time on your schedule, you can use that time to develop new customers who will pay you in trade dollars without affecting your cash income, creating an additional revenue stream. Professionals such as accountants, dentists and lawyers are just a few who regularly barter their services quite efficiently.

If you are selling products, unless you are turning away cash business, you may find that bartering turns out to be the best thing you've ever done for your business. For me, barter is in the top five life changing events I've experienced in more than thirty eight years of business, and I continue to reap the benefits of bartering on a daily basis.

Barter allows merchandise sellers the chance to reduce inventory, eliminate markdowns and increase sales, thereby improving profitability. Bartering also opens new doors allowing you to service more customers and to meet local business owners. You can take advantage of tax benefits with barter dollars in the same way you do when you spend cash. The difference is you unlock your dormant cash dollars by converting them to trade dollars, freeing up your money that is tied up in aged inventory, overstocks etc. This allows you to reduce cash expenses with your new found trade dollars, freeing up your actual cash to do something else with, thereby effectively improving your cash flow too.

New Revenue and Cash Flow

Barter also can increase your cash flow through new found revenue when your new barter customers, just like cash customers, become referral sources and bring you friends or relatives that spend cash with you. Sometimes a barter customer will also spend cash with you for things you do not wish to trade such as special orders, limited editions etc. Yes, just because you barter, doesn't mean you have to barter everything you offer, in fact, you should only barter in ways that benefit your business and certainly do not replace cash sales with barter sales, as the goal is always to supplement your cash sales.

I'll go into great detail later on about how to build new revenue but here is one simple example; a restaurant that barters on its off peak days such as Sunday through Thursday maximizes the value of its chef in the kitchen and wait staff on the floor by bringing in new customers in slow times. Since the actual product cost is relatively low in relation to the size of the sale and the payroll is not affected, any additional revenue will create an additional profit center. In addition the servers earn additional cash tips that make them happier to work for you. If new customers have an enjoyable dining experience they are very likely to recommend you to cash customers.

Another way barter can increase your cash flow is through tax savings, which is so important to understand that I've devoted a chapter for this that you should revisit after you begin trading. If you've been trading for a while, hopefully this chapter will give you some insight as to how to make your trade dollars work more intelligently for you.

When you accumulate trade dollars from your extra time or difficult to sell inventory it feels like new found money, because you've actually just created a new way to convert a stale asset into another asset that you can access more effectively. As your trading volume grows, you will also find this creates an opportunity to avail yourself of some extra perks that you couldn't otherwise afford or be comfortable purchasing if cash flow has been tight in your business.

Over the years, I have bartered everything from the mundane such as dry cleaning, apparel and show tickets to significant personal expenses, including the replacement of a deck on my house and a new driveway. I even purchased a revenue generating asset when I bought a rental income property. More often I am reducing business expenses by repaving a parking lot for my store, hosting holiday parties at amazing venues for my staff and doing so much more on trade!

An epiphany should take place when you start reducing your business expenses by using trade dollars and your cash dollars have fewer demands on them all around.

When done right, bartering will allow you to alter your lifestyle in a positive manner. The benefits appear in simple ways such as dining out more often or in more extravagant restaurants than normal. Benefits also come in larger ways and you might also find yourself going on an extravagant vacation, buying a fur coat or fine jewelry more often than you are accustomed to. These lifestyle changes evolve as you progress at trading and what used to be an extravagant notion can become within reach.

Cash Flow Relief

Converting traditional cash transactions to barter transactions may provide cash flow relief to a business that cannot meet its cash needs due to a short term lack of cash on hand, or a deepening cash flow crisis culminating in mounting debt. By converting cash expenses to trade transactions, the need to cut or reduce cash budgets may be eliminated. Since reducing budgets for items such as marketing, advertising and other expenses which are usually considered essential to stimulate growth might actually be harmful to a business, barter can be an effective management tool to avoid this.

An insolvent business may find the path to solvency through bartering its goods and services, freeing up cash to meet outstanding obligations, eventually contributing to the return to solvency and ultimately to greater cash flows and profitability.

If times are tough, barter can often provide enough reduction in cash expenditures to take you out of the red on your cash flow and get you into the black. The benefit here is the extra cash freed up by trading can be used to pay down debt, saving cash interest expense and carrying costs. In higher rate interest environments, the carrying costs of old inventory can escalate substantially, in terms of debt carrying costs and increased insurance premiums. High interest rates make it even more important to convert burdensome assets into something more useful. Once you start, it becomes like the proverbial ball rolling down the hill picking up momentum as it goes. Having goals and a plan can eliminate disappointments or remorseful feelings down the road.

NOT EVERY OPPORTUNITY, IS AN OPPORTUNITY

CHAPTER 3

WHY WOULDN'T YOU BARTER?

Admittedly, barter is not for everyone. In my mind, there are only three primary reasons you shouldn't be bartering:

1. If your cash business is so strong that you would lose cash sales in order to make a barter transaction.
2. You have no free time.
3. Your profit margins are too small to justify the costs of bartering.

If one of these applies to you, then barter probably wouldn't provide you with enough benefits to make it worth your effort. If you would lose cash sales to make trades then don't do it. If you have no free time you might actually be able to barter some services that currently consume your time and that's worth thinking about for all of us. And, if your profit margins are thin, you might do much better bartering goods for higher value than selling them for cash. When it comes to profit margins, a good rule of thumb to follow is, the higher your markup; the more aggressively you should be bartering goods and services.

Although not a new concept, barter is not an option many businesses people think about because they have been conditioned to operate their businesses in the traditional cash and carry manner. Much like the stuff in the back of your closet you forget about, you probably know about barter but haven't felt a need to put it to use. Also, some people just aren't driven to raise extra revenue or they value their time in a manner that prohibits them from anything that doesn't provide the immediate results that cash money can bring. If you have more money than you need and no time, then the benefits of bartering to make more money will be less appealing to you. Unfortunately, the latter scenario doesn't describe most of us.

As an example, if you are an extremely busy professional and your time and experience is what you rely on to earn a living, such as a dentist, with a practice that has no room on the schedule for another patient, you would be substituting barter credits for cash and clearly they are not the same. In this case the fees you would pay to a barter exchange and the limited membership where you could use your credits would probably not be beneficial for you.

However if the same dentist had several unfilled openings (pun intended) in their schedule on a regular basis, then bartering services would be extremely beneficial because there are almost no new costs associated with accommodating a barter customer. The fixed overhead for staff, utilities etc. is already in place. I've found that most businesses and professionals are never too busy to make an extra sale or offer services in slower periods. The key is to identify these periods of inefficiency and utilize them to provide benefits. Similarly, if you sell a product that has a limited supply which you sell out of consistently for cash; barter credits may not have value for you because they are being substituted for cash, not raising additional revenue.

Patience is a Virtue

Bartering typically requires more patience, flexibility and takes more time than a cash transaction, so if you are the "need it now" type of personality living in the fast lane, barter might frustrate you. Barter, especially in the early stages, before you develop personal contacts and know who you can contact directly to trade with, consumes more of your time and takes patience.

The need to contact your broker at a barter exchange to determine if they have the product or service you are looking for or when and where you might make a purchase adds an extra step in the purchasing process. The need to locate a printer to trade with can, but doesn't always, take more time than just visiting one of the many printers you know of around town. Therefore, thinking ahead will always yield better results and this will become second nature for you as you begin to trade more often. As discussed later, sometimes using a broker makes transactions easier.

If you needed a bicycle repaired, normally you might take it to a local store you pass on the way home every day and pay cash for a seventy five dollar repair. After you call the barter exchange, you may find they have a member who owns a bicycle shop that is located thirty minutes away from you in a direction not part of your normal travel routine. To travel thirty minutes and conserve the cash is great for some people and just not worth it to others who prefer simplicity in their lives or have the cash to spend.

Challenges

There are a few challenges that you should be aware of before venturing into the world of barter or joining a barter exchange. These can be described as the disadvantages of using trade dollars instead of cash dollars, but they are really challenges to work around.

In many instances bartering has fewer opportunities to purchase or sell goods and services compared to cash transactions because of several inherent limitations. These limitations include the inability to find a vendor willing to trade what you need and not enough members in an exchange to meet the demands of the membership. The reverse can also be true when there are too many members in your industry competing for the same business, preventing you from maximizing your ability to sell. However, the good news is these challenges only exist in a limited number of industries.

Often new members have expectations that they will be able to get specific things they want or need and when they find out their wish list can't be filled they become upset and/or disillusioned with the trading concept feeling they have credits they can't use. New members also expect pricing to be the same as cash for items they wish to purchase and sometimes find merchants have inflated prices and don't know how to deal with this. The concept of overpricing and the value of a bartered dollar are important concepts that have chapters devoted specifically to them.

Exchanges, regardless of their size, have a limited number of members, some may have a few hundred, while others have a few thousand or tens of thousands with a National or International presence, but they are still limited compared to how you can shop with your cash dollars. The advantage of your new found revenue source can be reduced to some degree based on the value you can find within an exchange's membership. These pitfalls and others you may happen upon are often avoided early in the interview process when learning about what different exchanges do and don't have to offer, thereby managing your expectations and making your barter experience more fruitful.

While vacation destinations are abundantly available on trade, including hotels for any budget and all-inclusive resorts, transportation to these venues is often limited and often is a cash expense. Airfare is one of the more difficult things to barter, but it does become available from time to time. Airfare can be included in a package or come in the form of a voucher with rules for use. Because of the limitations that come with vouchers, sometimes it's difficult or unlikely that the destination you have in mind will be available and if they were, the time frame in which you can use the vouchers may be limited, affecting your ability to use them. Yet vouchers work great for some traders.

I have traveled far and wide while enjoying awesome vacations on trade because I ask my broker what's available, rather than trying to get to a predetermined resort or country. If something my broker has sounds interesting, I'll take advantage of it. Of course the more specific you become in your request, the fewer options you may have to consider. I've travelled many times to Mexico, Jamaica and Europe on trade deals simply by being flexible, not to mention the many places in the United States I've been able to visit because hotels or resorts are readily available here.

My trip to Paris was not only a great deal from a cost perspective, but it also has provided my wife and me with a lifetime of memories. The money we saved on the hotel costs allowed us to enjoy some extravagances like dining at Jules Verne in the Eiffel Tower. That was sensational, and relatively expensive, but palatable!

Typically I would say something like "I want to go somewhere warm, hot would be better, between the weeks of…. and on a budget of about….. for two people". This flexibility lets a broker go into the marketplace and come back with several options to offer you and this approach has worked well for me.

Other destinations I've traveled to have included many places in the US from coast to coast and the Caribbean. This doesn't work if you have your heart set on taking the family to Disney during spring recess, which is the height of the vacation season; that's probably going to be a cash expense.

In my experience, airline vouchers are elusive as they become available to trade exchanges in large blocks and they are sold quickly unless you have a relationship with your broker who calls when they become available.

Special Orders are Difficult

Often a member will be frustrated because they can't order the items they want and have to settle for what merchants have in stock, making them feel their barter dollars aren't working for them, and they sour on the concept. Understanding why this happens will help you avoid this frustration.

A few of the primary advantages of barter for sellers are to improve cash flow and reduce inventory which is in direct conflict with the concept of filling special orders.

Since many merchants barter to conserve cash, the need to order new products to be bartered for credits creates a negative cash flow forcing the merchant to layout new money in return for credits that may accumulate in their account. This is a particularly poor idea if the vendor already has a significant trade balance on hand.

This doesn't mean no one will barter special orders; quite the contrary, many businesses sell the types of products that are specifically made to order, but it is less likely that seasoned traders who are bartering to reduce or manage their inventories will do so. There are members with a business model that do make items to order such as gift basket and chocolate companies or merchandising companies who will often do this for you, but even though the basket may be custom it's usually made from components the member has on hand. This is one of the challenges new members should be aware of when beginning to barter.

Rejection

On rare occasions you may be rejected for membership by an exchange. I have seen this in a local exchange where they already had a few dentists and would not accept new ones because they already knew there would not be enough business from the membership base to sustain an additional dentist. This is more likely to happen to a business that offers services rather than products, but is not common. Don't be upset or offended; just find another exchange that will welcome you.

Small Profit Margins

Do you know what your gross margin is? What is your actual cost to make a sale? If your profit margin is too thin, meaning your cost of goods is a large percentage of your selling price or your variable overhead required to complete a sale is significant, then barter might not be for you. Your fixed costs are already sunk and usually can't be removed from your cost of goods calculations but variable cost can be addressed and often reduced by bartering. Selling more units or services should lower your fixed costs per sale on an amortized basis as well.

A very small profit margin is ok in a business that has large sales volume. I know people who make a gross profit of one or two percent on sales but do millions of dollars in volume so they make a nice profit because they operate with very low expenses that don't erode their margins. Small profit margins usually make it difficult to create good barter scenarios. If you have small profit margins but are looking to convert overstocked products or other assets to another form of currency, then barter could still have benefits for you.

Wholesale vs. Retail

Wholesalers, by the very nature of their business model, generally have much smaller profit margins than retailers and service type businesses because they rely on volume and turnover to make their money. You might think the previous section titled "Small Profit Margins" would apply to wholesalers, but it shouldn't! The reason for this is a wholesaler can exercise the option of bartering at retail prices, as opposed to someone that has small profit margins as a result of rigid market values or conditions they don't control.

When wholesalers exercise barter transactions at retail prices they can achieve significantly greater profit margins and purchasing power when trading. Wholesalers should also focus on using this methodology to move out overstocks and aging merchandise. Some merchants do trade at their wholesale pricing and that's great for those of us that can take advantage of these opportunities to leverage our trade dollars. When this happens it's not really a level playing field for the seller. The reason for this is the seller will most likely have to convert those wholesale barter credits into retail purchases and will have far less purchasing power than those on the other side of those transactions.

A word of caution for wholesalers who are usually exempt from collecting sales tax; you may have to do so for certain types of retail sales, so be sure to check with your accountant before venturing into the retail side of your business.

Is It Worth the Effort?

While I suspect there may be a few more valid reasons for not bartering products or services, the benefits for most businesses will outweigh the disadvantages by far. Like many things in life, becoming accustomed with the nuances of trading may take a little time, but if you stick with it the results can be very rewarding. It's not a big learning curve and you will improve as you make more trades so don't be intimidated.

The inability to understand all of the benefits received by bartering prevents many from joining an exchange. Prospective barter members see the costs associated with joining an exchange and don't know if it is worth joining. If you manage your transactions to maximize your bottom line potential like I do, then I'm here to say, yes, it's well worth it!

SELF IMPOSED LIMITS ARE THE ONLY THING THAT LIMIT YOURSELF

CHAPTER 4

THE SKY IS THE LIMIT

The most significant barter deal on record is undoubtedly still the one in which early Dutch settlers traded with the native Indians: trading twenty four dollars' worth of iron wares and cloth, for the island of Manhattan. At the time Manhattan was largely unused and had no intrinsic value to those who traded it because land was plentiful. The Indians in essence, had more inventory than they needed. History has proved the Dutch used barter to their advantage, finding a trading partner who arguably undervalued what they were trading, but at the time, both parties had to agree it was a fair deal in order to conclude the transaction.

There are no limits, whether you trade millions of dollars in tiny transactions or have a big ticket item worth a million dollars or more. There are many experienced traders willing to make a direct swap or trade for credits with you. The challenge lies in your ability to locate a buyer and the next chapter opens the doors to connecting with thousands of trading partners around the country and throughout the world if you need to expand your search.

You are truly only limited by your imagination and determination to make a deal.

If you stop attempting to achieve your goals because you believe others who say it can't be done or have failed before you, then that only means you will abandon your chances of accomplishing what you might truly be capable of. So the sky is the limit, if you have to have one.

Income Property

When working with a barter customer in one of my stores, we came to talking about rental income properties. I owned a few houses I was renting at the time and my customer had one that he was having difficulty managing; to the point that he realized he wasn't cut out to be a landlord and he wanted out. He had just listed the property with a broker that promised him a great price, so he was trying to sell the house for cash like most of us would do. I suggested to him that if he was interested in trading a portion of his equity with me that I would be willing to take it off of his hands. A few months later he returned to ask if I was still willing to buy his house since he wasn't happy with any of the cash offers he was getting.

The terms of the deal were simple. I gave him a sizeable down payment in trade dollars and would finance the balance against the cash flow that the legal two family home was generating to create a "no money" down transaction for myself in terms of my cash outlay. What was astonishing to most people was that I convinced a bank to lend me the money on an investment property without putting up cash. I was able to accomplish this by finding a lender that was willing to recognize my down payment in trade credits as good and valuable consideration in lieu of cash. What allowed me to do *this* was the fact that my trade credits were held by a third party in a barter exchange account from whom

I received a 1099-B declaring them as income recognized by the IRS, which the bank then acknowledged as an acceptable source of funds in order to underwrite the loan.

I then improved the aging Victorian property I acquired, updating the battered roof, the crumbling driveway, painting it inside and out by using additional trade dollars, further conserving my use of cash and increasing my equity in the property substantially. I enjoyed the positive cash flow as a primary income from the property for several years while my tenants paid the mortgage down giving me my second revenue stream in the form of equity build up. I realized a third financial benefit because I was able to depreciate the cost of the property over the course of several years, thereby receiving tax savings in addition to the tax deductible repairs that were made to maintain the property. My fourth source of income was the most significant and was all cash when I sold the property for a substantial gain and reaped the rewards of appreciation. I then parlayed the cash from this property into a new real estate venture.

When I sold the property, the full amount of my barter deposit *plus* all of the trade dollars I sunk into repairs and maintenance of the property were recouped as non-taxable cash first because this increased my cost basis for tax purposes. This happens because my bartered equity was treated the same way as cash equity would be, returning it to an investor for accounting purposes. Whatever cash capital improvements I also made would become part of my cost basis as well. The remaining difference between my investment, less depreciation, and the sales price was my capital gain.

I probably never would have sold the property if it were not for the same reasons it was sold to me. The house was located within the incorporated Village of Patchogue, New York, which is a very difficult place to own a rental property because the Village doesn't want you there. The Village attempts to make landlords responsible for tenant's actions and creates discriminatory rules that don't apply to your neighbors that you must abide by as a landlord, if you want to obtain and maintain a rental permit. So like my predecessor, eventually I sold the property and moved on, but I sold it for cash with a nice capital gain.

Artwork

There is fine art and then there is art, artwork doesn't have to be valuable or an investment; it can simply be the perfect piece of décor to compliment your furnishings or something you appreciate. If it appreciates in value that's certainly a bonus! I have purchased many items in both categories to decorate my stores, office and home by bartering for them.

My favorite piece is a self-portrait done as an original etching by Rembrandt, the Master. I have accumulated some originals by Itzchak Tarkay, plus the works of many well-known names such as Thomas McKnight, Wayne Ensrud, Erte, and Sabzi. Whether your tastes flow to oil paintings, water colors, etchings, lithographs, bronzes, sculptures or any other art form, you will likely find more art available to trade for than you can imagine.

When shopping for artwork, if you can purchase it framed you will save the time and expense of doing it yourself. Also ask for paperwork stating authenticity and value at the time of purchase, which will save you the cash expense of obtaining appraisals later if you want to insure or ultimately sell an item. Much of the artwork I have purchased has been framed because I'm drawn to it as a complete piece, but some people do prefer to purchase unframed art and there is no need to worry about inheriting the cash expense of having it framed as there are also many businesses in the framing trade that will barter a custom frame for you. Instead of inheriting costs, you can start thinking about who might be inheriting your most recent acquisition.

Big Tickets

Much like purchasing art, when buying any big ticket item, it is prudent to obtain an appraisal whenever possible and verify value before closing the deal. Real estate, boats, autos and other big tickets are all traded for regularly. Ask up front for any additional documentation, warranties etc. so you have

them in the event you decide to resell an item. This will help

you maximize the return on your investment.

THE ROAD TO RICHES
IS A TOLL ROAD,
BE HAPPY TO PAY
THE FEE

CHAPTER 5

USING A BARTER EXCHANGE

Selecting an Exchange

Unless you have received a recommendation for an exchange, or want to contact one listed in the appendix, you can locate many simply by surfing the Web. A good place to start would be *NateBarter.com*, which stands for National Association of Trade Exchanges. Nate's members are independently owned barter organizations from all over that adhere to "standards of ethics and integrity used to maintain federal compliances and regulations."

You can use Google to research exchanges in your area and look up any of the *National Barter Exchanges*. You will find a wealth of resources without much effort. If you happen to live on Long Island, N.Y., I would highly recommend these two local exchanges with national contacts; *Tradeworks* and

NCE (National Commerce Exchange). I have done business with both of these companies for many years and have found them to be great to deal with. Contact information for Tradeworks and NCE can be found in the appendix.

Ask the Right Questions

After doing your research and selecting an exchange that looks right for you, it's time to set up an interview.

This is the time to ask questions and negotiate for discounts, exclusivity or other things that may be important to you.

It's tough to make a decision when you don't know what questions to ask, so ask open ended questions and get the person you are interviewing to talk. What they say will prompt you to ask more questions and make more informed decisions. Make a list of questions to work from so you gather as much information as you can in your first discussion.

Ask to see a copy of their membership agreement and read it. Highlight things that are objectionable and see if you can negotiate them. This will be incrementally harder with larger exchanges than the smaller ones. Small exchanges will value the chance to do business with you more than adhering to the fine print. The larger exchanges love the fine print because their attorneys have drafted it to afford them as many protections as they can in the event you violate their rules.

In my experience the size of an exchanges membership correlates directly to the value you will receive from it. Avoid small or very new exchanges to begin with. Exchanges with a small membership base will probably struggle to meet your needs to make purchases and in some instances cannot provide enough outlets for your product or services. Exchanges with a thousand members exist and obviously can meet more of your needs. Different exchanges have strengths and weaknesses in their membership. Some exchanges, usually national ones, have excellent travel packages available and often hard to find items like real estate or vehicles. Every exchange I have ever contacted offers basic business services and personal or home improvement services.

Also make a list of items you use regularly or would like to acquire so you can determine if the exchange can fulfill your needs. Go through your checkbook and determine what reoccurring expenses you have that you might be able to barter. This is the most effective way to reduce your outgoing cash and increase your buying power. Ask questions like: How many hair salons do you have? Instead of: Do you have a hair salon?

Because exchanges are made up of businesses they are a great place for accountants to create new relationships. A recent email I received from an exchange promoting accountants listed fifteen tax preparers as members. In relation to the size of the membership this may seem excessive but wouldn't matter if the members are meeting each of their needs, yet as an accountant you would want to be aware of this.

The kinds of questions you will want to ask will arise as you read further on but here's a head start on your list:

Interview questions:

How long have you been in business?

How many people work in your office?

How many members do you have?

Do you have any members that offer _____?

(Insert your product or services)

If so, how many and where are they located?

How many offices do you have?

Where are they located?

Will I have a broker assigned to me?

Do you assign staff to departments?

Do you have a website I can buy and sell from?

Do you host a trade show or have merchandise available from your office?

Do you have reciprocal relationships with other exchanges?

Can you send me a list of the media that you have available?

I'm interested in travelling, can you tell me what packages you have available now?

Will you allow me to make purchases before I start selling?

Ask open ended questions:

What are your strengths?

What are your weaknesses?

How do you feel my products (or services) will be received by your members?

What are your fees?
The response you get is always followed by this question:

Are there any other fees?

Items on your wanted list to get details about:

Business services – copy machines/repairs etc.

Professional services – legal, accounting, advertising

Personal interests - vacations, art, jewelry etc.

Personal services - dry cleaning, hair salons etc.

Restaurants

Entertainment

Avoid New Brokers

I hate to say it and have a harder time writing it because I

truly believe everyone deserves a chance to succeed, but it

shouldn't necessarily be at your expense; "avoid new brokers", there, I said it. In the process of interviewing an exchange you should inquire about how many staff members they have and how long they have been with the exchange. If they intend to assign someone new to the exchange to your account, then ask if they have a background in trading elsewhere. Find out who is the top dog in sales for their office, that's who you want working for you.

Your broker is the key to accessing the membership and pushing great deals your way, deals that often come from years of working with others to develop those leads that you will want to come your way. You are joining an exchange to improve *your* bottom line and if you are new to trading and don't know what to ask you may become the victim of inefficiency.

Companies with staff need to hire new people and train them, so do I, but the new kid on the block, regardless of how nice they seem or well-meaning they are, just can't produce the results you want from day one and you will never know what you are missing. Try to engage the most experienced trader in the office as part of your agreement when signing on if you are not going to be dealing with the owner of a small exchange and are serious about pursuing barter.

Bookkeeping

Think of your barter exchange as a clearing house for purchases and sales. When you make a purchase it is "charged" to your account and the exchange acts just like a credit card company, recording your transactions on a monthly statement. When you sell, the same thing happens, but unlike a credit card processing company, the funds don't end up in your bank account, they stay with the exchange as "credits" that appear on the same monthly statement. These credits will be applied against current purchases or balances due and the remainder is available for you to spend in the future. Therefore, one of the primary functions of a trade exchange is bookkeeping or accounting. A trade exchange also issues a 1099-B form to each of its members at the end of the year for tax purposes. Form 1099-B shows the amount of sales you made for the previous calendar year.

Like a credit card you have a revolving balance that adjusts every time you buy or sell something, but unlike a credit card, instead of only building debt, you can also build a positive balance when your sales (credits) accumulate at a greater rate than your purchases (debits). I have built positive trade balances in excess of a hundred thousand dollars at times, knowing I would have use for these funds in the future.

Forms of Barter Currency

Barter is a form of currency, which changes hands in several forms that facilitate bookkeeping for exchanges and makes it easier to complete transactions. Members are usually issued ID cards that may resemble plastic credit cards. These cards can be used to make purchases from fellow members; the merchant manually fills out a two part slip like the old credit card slips. Sometimes business card style ID's are used and some exchanges provide customers with actual checks they can write to make purchases. Punch cards purchased in predetermined increments of one hundred dollars or so may also be used, eliminating the need for authorizations on multiple small dollar transactions. Punch cards are commonly issued for merchants that you would typically visit often, like an ice cream store where they would punch the corresponding number of holes for every dollar you spend. Gift certificates may be issued by exchanges or merchants to reduce the need for authorizations. You might also come across an exchange that issues scrip, which is the exchanges own paper money that can be exchanged for goods or services with other vendors.

Credit Line

Exchanges also offer credit lines. In many instances a trade exchange will offer you a nominal credit line to get started. I've seen this range from two thousand to ten thousand dollars, but the sky is the limit based on your creditworthiness and an exchange's confidence in extending you a credit line.

Broker

You will most likely be assigned a trade broker who will work with you and guide you through the process of buying and selling. In smaller exchanges you might deal directly with the owner of the exchange. Brokers have dual representation in most transactions since they are usually working for the buyer and seller.

Newsletter and Email Blasts

Read the newsletters and email blasts your exchange sends out to learn about new members and changes that will help you become a better trader. This is also a great way promote your business for free, so submit an offer to promote a product or service as often as you can and as often as the exchange will allow you to.

Travel

In addition to booking travel or a vacation on barter, you can sometimes shop while away because many barter exchanges have multiple offices or relationships with other exchanges, making it easy to find local businesses at many travel destinations. I bought some artwork in St. Thomas from an exchange member while cruising in the Caribbean. I just wrote a barter check and brought home a great vacation souvenir!

How Much Should I Trade?

Over time you will develop a sense of how many trade dollars you can buy and sell to keep a comfortable balance in your trade account. Figure out how much you plan to spend monthly and carry a balance of two or three times that so you are prepared to take advantage of any unforeseen deal just beyond the horizon that may come your way. If an exchange is meeting your needs, you will become comfortable accumulating larger balances. If an exchange isn't meeting your needs, you should have a conversation with the exchange's owner or manager to discuss your expectations. If you don't achieve the results you desire after your discussion, then move to an exchange that's more attentive to your needs.

Whenever possible, new members should make a few purchases before making any significant sales.

This can be accomplished by using a credit line the exchange grants you when signing up, or by creating limited initial sales followed by purchases to get a feel for how the system works. It may take you some time to absorb the different pace of trading compared to cash transactions. The primary benefit of doing this is you will not oversell and then become dismayed if you cannot spend your credits at the pace you would like to. This will give you the ability to get a sense of how you should balance your buying and selling on trade and make you a happier trader.

Fees

Barter exchanges make their money by charging fees for the services they offer while bringing buyers and sellers together. Exchange fees or commissions are usually a percentage of sales. Ten percent is a benchmark. I've paid as low as a five or six percent commission rate and as much as twelve percent, which I found to be too high for me and I ended up using other sources instead. While fees are one of those things that none of us like to pay, I have always rationalized that they really are a form of an advertising expense since I joined an exchange to attract new customers and new business. It's also important to acknowledge that when exchanges provide good leads and work for you, they have their own overhead and need to collect these fees to continue to provide the valuable services they offer.

Fees can be assessed in several ways. Using a ten percent fee structure as an example, more often than not, the ten percent would be charged to the buyer when making a purchase. The reason assessing the buyer with the full ten percent fee works best is twofold; the buyer is receiving goods or services for their credits and happy to pay the relatively small cash fee because a need is being fulfilled in a positive manner. If the buyer is getting three thousand dollars in new carpet for his office installed, the three hundred dollar commission seems inconsequential when compared to the cash he is not laying out to purchase the carpet. The seller on the other hand generates a receivable in a sales transaction and adding a fee negatively impacts the seller's cash flow at a time where they are *giving* not *receiving* to create a transaction. Some exchanges will split the fee as five percent to the buyer and five percent to the seller in a transaction, still collecting a full ten percent but affecting the members' cash flow differently. Other arrangements also exist.

Additionally, experienced traders like me do not mind selling to accumulate trade balances in our accounts if we can do so without incurring cash fees to accomplish this. If I sell fifty thousand dollars of stale inventory and convert it into trade dollars that sit dormant in my account for a while I don't mind. This is ok because I know I will use the credit at some point in the future and not having a carrying cost to convert the inventory into a more useful asset appeals to me. If I had to pay the ten percent fee up front, I would have to take five thousand hard cash dollars out of my business to change that inventory to credit and it would be highly unlikely that I would do that. Exchanges have no problem with this because as brokers they make a commission in every deal; it's simply a matter of who's paying it to them. They also know if I accumulate credits, eventually I will spend them down so it's money in the bank for them as well.

Members who fail to pay the fees on their accounts at some point will have their accounts *frozen* by an exchange, which means they will not have access to their credits to spend until they make their past due balance current again.

Other Fees

Most exchanges charge monthly fees in cash and/or in trade dollars. One of my exchanges bills me some trade dollars every month and ten dollars in cash to maintain my account. Frankly I never asked why a portion is in trade. With thousands of members, they collect hefty trade dollars that I assume they use to acquire things they need to operate their business and offer additional compensation to their staff too. You might see a recurring annual fee in addition to or instead of a monthly fee. Fees are due in cash; but when traders use the term cash it usually means cash, company check, money order, credit card or other monetary instrument that is not barter. Sometimes having an automatic credit card payment agreement on file with an exchange induces them to offer a lower fee because they don't have to expend any effort to collect their money and this improves their cash flow.

Special Fees

In an effort to offer extra services or benefits to their clients, some trade exchanges have brokers assigned to specific categories like travel arrangements or advertising. These brokers are specialists in these areas and the exchange may charge an additional fee for their concierge type service over and above the regular commission rate or instead of their standard commission rate. I've been able to avoid most of these additional charges by working with other exchanges offering similar services without additional fees, yet on some occasions a special vacation may come my way and I'm happy to pay the up charge.

Other Cash Expenses

In addition to exchange fees and sales tax, as a buyer you would normally be expected to pay cash for things that do not have profit margins such as gratuities, shipping, alterations etc. Even though these things are usually the buyer's responsibility, vendors may include some of these costs on trade, which only makes your deal sweeter.

Members Are Vetted

Another advantage to using an exchange is that members are vetted in the application process where the exchange confirms they are a registered business with a tax ID. They get to know the member and have significant leverage they can use to protect other members because they control the funds in the trading accounts. The exchange provides you with a source of recourse if you run into an unscrupulous member. Trade exchanges can and do expel members who violate their rules repeatedly, commit a major infraction or do something illegal.

Recourse

Recourse is defined as a source of help or a means of resolving disputes and a barter exchange can offer you recourse as a third party. An exchange's ability to protect your interests is a significant benefit they offer. Exchanges have relationships with their customers who they can work out solutions to problems and challenges with, but more importantly they control the purse strings. Exchanges can arbitrate or settle disputes on your behalf and can escrow or withhold funds in a transaction to insure you get paid. Some of the powers an exchange has should be outlined in your member agreement.

Authorizations

A significant benefit provided by exchanges is the authorization process they offer that insures you will be guaranteed payment if you properly authorize a sale; much in the same way as a credit card authorization works.

Exchanges usually have a twenty four hour phone number you can call to get automated authorizations, but some of the smaller exchanges may still do authorizations in person via the phone.

American Express says "Membership has its advantages". And while doing business with customers you know may allow for the extension of certain courtesies, getting paid is of paramount importance. In order to protect yourself; even though you may know your buyer, you should always go through the approval process. Never ship or give out merchandise without an authorization from your exchange.

If your exchange is closed on weekends, holidays etc., you can charge the purchase to a credit card, and refund the customer after you have received barter exchange approval with the understanding if you cannot get the approval, the transaction will convert to a cash sale (credit card) or the item will be returned depending on your business's policy. Obviously services rendered can't be returned.

If the size of the transaction is a small amount or you know the customer, you always have the option of taking a calculated risk that you will be able to obtain the authorization. In order to avoid these situations, if you know a customer is coming in when the regular authorization process is not available, you or your customer can request the exchange to pre-authorize a sale, which they will gladly do if a client is in good standing.

Refunds and Returns

The need to make a return or issue a refund will eventually arise if you become an active trader. Credits are usually handled the same way credit card purchases are in terms of accounting. Any applicable fees paid by the buyer or seller to the exchange are refunded to the parties by the exchange in a normal transaction. If a deal goes bad with an exchange member, who refuses to issue a refund legitimately due or procrastinates in doing so, then getting a refund you are entitled to is simplified because you have the exchange operating as an intermediary insuring you are credited properly. You can communicate through your broker rather than dealing with a difficult or hostile member as exchanges often assist in settling disputes between members.

PICK UP THE PHONE
AND REQUEST
MORE CUSTOMERS

CHAPTER 6

USING AN EXCHANGE TO YOUR ADVANTAGE

Money to Go Please!

Yes, you can order additional business and new customers too! Pick up the phone and call your broker to request additional customers. Your broker will find them for you and send them to your place of business. Surprisingly, barter exchanges also offer access to products and services you might not find or be exposed to when spending cash. Imagine having a new sales representative without payroll costs that sends business your way for a nominal fee. That's what trade brokers do, they just don't think of the service they provide that way. More often brokers are motivated by the commission they get when you buy something.

Your Trade Broker

When you join most exchanges, you are assigned a trade broker. Your trade broker is a very important contact and you should work at developing the best relationship you can with them. As I just alluded to, by viewing your broker as a sales rep and consciously using your broker to send you customers on a continuous basis, you will be able to reap rewards far greater than the complacent members of an exchange.

Really get to know your broker, who is the gatekeeper at the trade exchange and has access to all of the client databases.

Brokers know about the newest items and members as well as who is actively trading and who you could benefit from doing business with. A great relationship will afford you the opportunity to call in a *favor* when needed most and may just give you that edge you need to make a deal. Trade brokers also often have access to other exchanges or at least a relationship with someone in the office who has that access.

To improve your efficiency and maximize your potential within the barter community you should send a list of your wants and needs to your broker on a regular basis. Think ahead, the more time you can allow your broker to work on something out of the ordinary, the more successful they will be. As odd as it sounds, don't ever forget, to your trade exchange and broker, you are a CASH customer because that's how you pay your fees.

Your broker is also a free form of promotion for your business. Don't assume they know everything about your business, take some time to educate them so they can speak about you and your company intelligently; which will also aide your broker in identifying future prospects for you as requests for services and products come across the broker's desk. You've got a sales agent within your broker that can represent you; so figure out how to tap this new resource and help your broker to help you find more business.

Databases and Exchange Networks

Each exchange keeps track of the types of goods and services their members offer in databases or contact manager programs, so you need to do two things with your broker. First in order to sell most efficiently, you need to compile a detailed list of the services you offer and pass it on to your broker. Do not assume the broker understands your business or the nuances of segments within your business. For example as a jeweler my description could be: Fine jewelry, Gold, Silver Diamonds and Jewelry Repair Services. While most people think they know what a jeweler does and this may sound adequate, this is a woefully weak description for a broker to work with.

Let's take just the category of "Jewelry Repair" as an example. In order to assist your broker, so they can send you business, you need to help them understand that "Jewelry Repair" is a very diverse segment of your business. Just this category includes many items and services that you offer which might not immediately come to mind for someone not familiar with the inner workings of your business or trade. A better list that would more completely describe jewelry repair would look something like this:

Jeweler on Premises

Repairs done while you wait AND while you watch (As time permits)
This eliminates the need to worry about your valuables when you do business with us!
Custom work and special orders – designs made from our ideas or yours!
Remodeling services – turn your old and unwanted jewelry into new designs
Handmade jewelry from your precious metals or ours
Ring sizing, broken chain repairs, clasps replaced, gemstones reset and more...
Jewelry refinishing services – make your old jewelry look like brand new again
Antique jewelry restoration services – we fix the oldest and most unusual items
We repair all types of fine jewelry made from platinum, gold or silver
We repair fashion and costume jewelry
Watch batteries and replacement bands installed
Laser repairs on delicate items like opal and pearl jewelry
Pearl restringing – all types of beads restrung!
Engraving – monograms and inscriptions of all kinds added to our items or yours
Plating services – tarnished finishes on plated items refinished and re-plated like new
Appraisal and lab report services

Watch crystals replaced – we custom re-cut any scratched, chipped or broken glass
Watch dials refinished – rusty or pitted dials on an heirloom timepiece can be redone
Watches repaired – we service almost every brand made and warranty our work

Don't forget to include things like store hours, extra locations and anything that sets you apart from others in your field or industry. The smallest detail might prompt a significant sale so invest some time in this task.

Second: go through your checkbook and provide your broker with a list of items you buy regularly and create a wish list, which will allow your broker to refer members to meet your needs or locate items from other sources. Nothing is better about bartering than finding a source for something you buy regularly for cash and being able to barter for it so you can use the cash for something else. This is an ideal way to improve your cash flow.

Online Bartering

While most, if not all, exchanges now have websites, the more proactive ones have their own interactive web sites where you can purchase products online from the comfort of your own home or business. The exchange will provide you with a username and password to access the site. These sites can also authorize the sale and collect sales tax plus shipping if applicable, using the familiar shopping cart and checkout procedures found in other e-commerce sites. In addition to buying this way, you could be selling this way!

Your Own Web Page

If you have your own web site, then you can use it to trade your products or services, making them available to barter with members around the country. Because we target specific merchandise to trade in our business, we have developed private or hidden pages on our site for our barter customers.

Hidden pages are those that cannot be accessed from links within a website; you need to know the exact address of the page to connect directly to them. Since I manage my own web site, I do this by posting items to hidden pages, allowing me to separate the items we want to trade from our other merchandise. This makes it easier for potential customers to navigate to the right place and avoids confusion with respect to what items are available on a full trade basis. I can also post trading rules, shipping fees and other information of interest to barter customers in this barter section that the general public doesn't need to be exposed to when visiting my site to make cash purchases, thereby segregating these two types of transactions online.

I promote the items I have to trade by sending the link for the hidden pages to my brokers who distribute it to their clients, usually via email and within minutes I can have orders. One and a half minutes is my record time from sending an email to a broker who forwarded it to the members, until a member responded with a request to make a purchase. Not quite the speed of light, but very impressive nonetheless. This underscores the point I've made elsewhere about it being easier for me to barter products for trade dollars than sell them for cash and why I have selling limits or restrictions that you may not find the need to impose. If I have only an item or two, I just send some photos in an email to my brokers and achieve the same results as sending links to my web pages.

Repair Services

Because we have jewelers on our premises, we focus a lot of our marketing on this service in our stores where customers can wait and watch their valuables being repaired. Having a full service repair shop sets us apart from the competition and all of the businesses that only sell jewelry. As a result of this, customers that buy jewelry from on line sites with limited services, department stores, boutiques and the like need a place to have their items sized, altered, engraved etc. and we benefit from the opportunity to meet their customers' needs when we service what they sell. Because jewelry is of such a personal nature, this service makes people more comfortable doing business with us This also allows us to build on these relationships and we make many new customers by servicing jewelry sold by other retailers.

In addition to trading jewelry online, we also get inquiries about bartering jewelry repairs. It never really occurred to us to promote mail order repairs because of the sensitivity we felt people would have about shipping their jewelry to an unknown place for service. We have now realized that some people just don't have readily available access to a quality jeweler or simply would prefer to trade for the services; imagine that!

Barter customers have a level of comfort when shipping us their valuables because of the relationships they have with their barter exchanges and their ability to get references and learn about our reputation from others before doing business with us. The ability to have your reputation precede your introduction to a new client is another very valuable benefit of working with trade exchanges that makes it easier for you to close sales. Think about nontraditional ways you might grow your business through barter like we did because mail order jewelry repairs was never something we pursued before, but we do now!

Personal Shopper

I have always used my trade brokers as personal shoppers and you should too! It's a relationship really worth forging.

Because brokers work on commissions, they will appreciate it when you give them opportunities to work for you. As I have said, time is money, so use your broker to save you time and make you more money.

In addition to a wish list of things you would like to buy, think about what you may need for gifts or might have to buy in the near future. When needs arise to entertain guests, make travel arrangements or obtain tickets etc.; empower your broker to provide you with options. Your broker will then sift through their databases, check other exchanges and sources to see if they can fill your requests. Sometimes they will even have their sales people try to sign up a new member that offers what you need. A broker may even offer a potential new client the opportunity to do business with you to encourage them to sign up. Trade exchanges appreciate leads for people you might like to do business with as well. Many exchanges offer incentives ranging from credits to cash in an effort to stimulate leads and some have held contests to motivate members to grow their ranks.

Many years ago one of my brokers, a.k.a. my personal shopper, called me to say she found something she thought I could really use and wanted to let me know about it before she offered it to her other clients in the jewelry business and retail trades. It was a contact for a fellow that had jewelry sized gift boxes he was willing to trade. The deal turned out to be in the top ten trades I've ever made but had a funny twist, funny now, but not so funny for my staff at the time. I learned this seller had multiple sizes of gift boxes, some of which were identical to the ones I was already using in my stores. There is no better trade than when you can barter for something you are already buying for cash, allowing you to keep your greenbacks for other uses, so I was very interested.

At the time, these boxes cost me between fifty cents and a dollar each from my regular vendors. As it turns out, this fellow bought the boxes as a closeout very cheaply and just wanted to get rid of them to make room in his warehouse since he wasn't in the business of selling jewelry boxes. He was willing to trade them for a little less than the wholesale price I was paying, which although unusual, was a great opportunity for me and does happen when people acquire things they just want to unload quickly.

In our initial discussion I realized he would be pretty flexible, which opened the door for a spirited negotiation. Even though this was already a great deal for me, my "A" type personality always drives me to make the best deal possible and I saw an opportunity here to make a good bargain better. We negotiated down, well below his original asking price, to about ten cents apiece if I would take all of them in one shot.

He was very happy to unload them all quickly, having to make only one delivery rather than shipping a lot of small orders. Remember, time is money and very often much more valuable than products to people.

The total was just about ten thousand dollars, which was about five to ten times greater than what I would normally spend on a typical box order at that time, but I didn't have to come up with the cash, so I said I would take the lot. I was also getting five to ten times the product I would normally get for every dollar I spent. It sounded like a good idea at the time☺. A few days later a truck driver came into my store when I wasn't in and said he had a box delivery for us. My store manager asked him to bring them in and put them on the floor behind the register for her.

The driver looked around the store and said "I don't think you understand; I have *a lot* of boxes for you." So the manager said he could put them behind the counter against the wall and the driver responded – "No, I mean I have twenty pallets in a tractor trailer outside ~~for you~~, they're going to fill up most of your store." So that's what we did, needless to say there was total chaos for a little while until we split them up between our other stores and put some in our attics and basements.

To this day I still have a few cases of these boxes in my attic. If you haven't done the math yet, I bought about a hundred thousand boxes, and I saved about $65,000.00 in cash without spending any cash! Technically, I saved more because my ten thousand dollars in barter had a lower cash cost to me as well. If I had to come up with anywhere near the $75,000 in cash the boxes were worth, it never would have made sense, but barter dollars and a barter connection from my broker allowed me to buy into a mega deal. This was leveraging my buying power at its best, and of course I was able to deduct the cost of the boxes as an expense on my tax return; win, win, win!

Special or Limited Offers to Move Stock

When you have something to move, call your broker, they will work to find you a buyer. I would send my brokers emails with a specific item I wanted to sell for trade credits rather than marking it down in my store and waiting for someone to buy it.

Mark downs usually result in selling a discounted item instead of something else in your business with better profit margins, thereby reducing your profitability and sometimes your cash flow when a customer settles for a lower priced bargain instead of paying retail pricing for something else.

Your broker will also help you sell personal items or items not typically associated with your business. Maybe you have golf clubs you never used; they could even be used, your broker usually doesn't care, they can find you a buyer. Experienced brokers are intrigued by the art of a deal, they enjoy making transactions happen, make them smile!

Maximize Your Time

Make appointments to maximize the use and value of your time while preventing members from visiting unannounced and pulling you away from other tasks that may require your attention when they arrive. Having the freedom to focus on customers by appointment will allow both of you to have a better experience.

As your experience and understanding of trading improves you will be able to train one or more staff members to handle barter customers, increasing your potential and increasing their productivity.

Putting Your Account on Hold

At any time you feel you have sold enough goods or services and don't want to increase your account balance any further you can place your account "*on hold*". When you do this, your broker makes a note in the company's database to let other brokers know not to send you new business until the hold is lifted. A hold can be limited to a busy or seasonal time, which we do in the month of December. Although it sounds illogical at first to stop trading when people want to buy, we just become too busy handling our cash business. Our staff can't handle the extra time required to work with trade customers because we typically do forty percent of our annual business in the end of the fourth quarter and must capitalize on every opportunity to raise cash.

Even though we have the ability to accrue more barter dollars than we need at other times of the year, we do have to make accommodations when on hold that are good for business. We fit in an occasional barter customer here and there and will return a *favor* we owe a broker. We also will fill a desperate request from a trading partner or a regular trade customer that visits us all year. However, these are benefits members that have developed great relationships with us or their broker receive. You may be surprised to learn that we do still offer items during our peak seasons from our website. Because we can pack and ship orders when we get a break during busy days and it has virtually no impact on our ability to conduct our cash business, this makes sense for us.

Fees

Like everything in life, except death and taxes, fees are negotiable; negotiate the fees the exchange charges BEFORE you open an account. Exchanges usually charge a sign-up fee, which among other things covers the commission they pay a sales rep to sign you on and possibly a referral fee they may be passing on to a member that introduced you to the exchange. Often you can get the one time sign-up fee waived if the exchange feels you could be a good member for them or if you contact the owner or manager of an exchange and sign up directly, saving them the cost of sending someone out to recruit you.

After you've been a member of an exchange for a while, if you find you are doing significant business with the exchange, you can attempt to renegotiate your fee based on the volume of business you are bringing to the exchange. While doing so, remind your exchange if you have referred several new members and be sure to emphasize the value you offer them as a member. The cost of doing business with you decreases proportionately for an exchange as the trading you do increases in volume.

You will never get what you do not ask for.

If you can get your rate reduced by only one percent, say from ten to nine percent, then that represents a ten percent reduction in the actual cash fees you pay. In other words if you hit the one hundred thousand dollar mark in sales, you would reduce your normal cash fees from ten thousand dollars to nine thousand dollars and put a thousand dollars back in your pocket while still allowing the exchange to make a significant profit on your account. When I renegotiated a six percent fee down to five percent, that one point saved me twenty percent of my now lower actual cash expenses

New Members

Frankly, new members aren't going to be a savvy as seasoned traders; and while I'm not advocating you should take advantage of new members, there are certain benefits to doing business with them. New members may have products not previously offered by other members so it's not uncommon for there to be higher than normal demand for their offerings, causing the new merchant to become overwhelmed or go into a "hold" status quicker than you might expect. Having a good relationship with your broker often gets you the first opportunity to work with new members that you might not otherwise even know about. This gives you the chance to cherry pick through their inventory ahead of the rush when the "Welcome new members" announcement goes out.

New members also tend to have very fairly priced products that reflect true cash values. They make fair barter transactions and offer most everything in their inventory as opposed to seasoned traders who may set stricter parameters that benefit their business and maximize their barter potential. Get to new members first on the premise the early bird gets the worm and you don't miss out.

Promoting Your Exchange

You might have an opportunity to promote an exchange you work with. ITEX, which is a large international barter exchange with many offices in the United States, offers a credit for promoting their exchange in your print advertising. If you use their logo indicating you are an ITEX member, then the amount of space used to display their logo may be well worth the credits you receive. This benefits ITEX in raising awareness of their brand name and notifying the public that you are a member of their organization. Their goal is to find potential members using your database or advertising.

Think you're ready? Of course you are, but where to start? Start by looking for a strong local exchange and a strong regional or national exchange.

IT'S TIME
TO THINK
DIFFERENTLY
ABOUT HOW YOU
GO SHOPPING

CHAPTER 7

BUYING AT TRADE SHOWS

Most barter exchanges host one or more *Trade Shows* each year, often held right before or during the holiday shopping season. Some trade shows can be elaborate in size in rented arenas while others may be special shopping days where the barter exchange turns its offices into a showroom filled with items for its members to purchase. Trade shows bring buyers and sellers together in a friendly atmosphere that simplifies transactions because everything is available "full trade" and no cash is needed to shop. If you see something you like, you just sign for it. Cash would only change hands if you are in a state that has a sales tax; then the appropriate tax would be paid to the selling vendor in cash.

Working the Room

If you are the timid type; this is not the time or place to be shy, it's time to deploy the aggressive forces within you and snap up the bargains, strike up conversations and dare to step out of your comfort zone. It's not every day you get to go on a shopping spree without having to use your credit card or spend cash money. It's time to think differently than you normally do about shopping.

Don't buy what you need now or for the next week, think more globally and be prepared with a list of what you might use in the coming year. How many birthday gifts will you need to buy in the next twelve months? How many items can you find to use as incentives to stimulate growth in your business over the next four quarters. What anniversaries fall within the next three hundred and sixty five days? How much cash did you spend last holiday shopping season that you could save this year by using your trade credits?

There are even vendors at shows whom we speak with prior to the event so they will bring things we have an interest in. Don't worry if you buy so much stuff that you will need to put an extension on your house to store it all because you can also barter with someone to get much of that work done too.

The first rule of trade show shopping is to arrive early, when the doors open if you can.

You MUST do this if you're serious about maximizing your day. The trendiest items, best bargains and items with very limited quantities will go fast. The check-in desk is the first place to start shopping! Ask if they have gift certificates available for restaurants or tickets to shows. These always go to those who arrive early and know to ask because they are very limited in dollar value and represent one of the great *cash dollar* for *trade dollar* values in bartering. Consider buying four or more tickets to a show you are interested in or some gift certificates to a restaurant so you can invite your favorite clients to join you; then write the whole evening off as a business expense at tax time.

How Things Change Hands

Members are usually screened at the door by the exchange to insure they are current in their accounts. One exchange I work with that hosts trade shows issues color coded passes or ID's to members when they check in. A green pass means the member has no spending limit, yellow means vendors should get an authorization over a specified dollar limit before completing a sale, and a red code means vendors should authorize all purchases.

One reason the exchange does this is to limit some members from spending well above their credit limits while not having every merchant approve every transaction which would be a cumbersome task with the amount of transactions made at these types of shows. This also makes it easier for sellers to process transactions in a simplified manner allowing them to do more business. The exchange's staff is on the floor checking on vendors to make approvals when needed throughout the event. Free food is a bonus often offered by the exchange. The exchange makes a deal with food merchants, who are usually happy to showcase samples of their offerings to encourage members to visit their businesses.

I love trade shows because I always fill the SUV with gifts for my customers, staff and wife. My wife loves trade shows because in addition to all of the shopping she can do for our business, there are always one or more furriers or high end apparel vendors. This allows us to make a big ticket purchase for ourselves every holiday season using our barter dollars.

If it were not for the extra barter revenue stream we have, we probably would not have accumulated the number of designer items we have acquired over the last few years. I usually find some nice apparel for myself too, including nice leather goods, shirts, and sweaters. There are always lots of ties to choose from. Small appliances, jewelry, handbags and electronics are a few of the categories that have always been abundantly available at the shows I've attended.

When venturing out to a trade show, in addition to starting early, if the venue is not too large, you should breeze through the room quickly and make mental notes of the big ticket vendors you might want to visit and any others that offer a potential for you to spend a significant sum. Also look for new merchants with products you haven't had the opportunity to buy before. This is important because when you walk the aisles vendor by vendor you tend to spend a lot of time talking to people, meeting new people, or buying small things and before you know it that first half hour gets lost to the veterans who already have bought out all of the inventory the chocolate lady had or the gift basket booth to fill their truck.

On that note, bring the biggest vehicle you have, just in case you find lots of deals too good to pass up. Remember, some business owners may have twenty, fifty or even more employees they are looking to barter gifts for. The furrier may only have one coat that you would be interested in and nothing is worse than seeing someone else wearing it and signing their barter slip as you approach. The later it gets in the day, the slimmer the pickings get for certain items and you end up settling for the best that's left without even knowing it. Some vendors are sold out by lunch time and are gone before the latecomers arrive. There's usually an evening crowd that comes down after work so the buying frenzy rebuilds for the vendors that are still well stocked.

For these reasons I work a show the way I do. I have the vendors hold what I paid for and pick it up when I'm done shopping, this way I can load the car before the show closes and all of the vendors are trying to load out. Then I visit the food vendors to get something to eat and don't mind if breakfast is gone. Some members head for the free food first, believing that's the best value of the day. I'd prefer to buy my own lunch rather than squander the opportunity to make a few thousand dollars in trade deals for the day.

If I can spend more than twenty thousand dollars at a trade show that I can use for my business and receive tax deductions for, it was a good day. If my wife gets to make a significant personal purchase it's a better day! I'm never as happy to spend money as I am when it's barter dollars because I know its money I never would have if I only did business for cash.

Traveling to Save Money

When you belong to large trade exchanges that have offices around the country, they will have multiple trade shows that may be worth traveling to. As an example, ITEX has trade shows in several states hosted by the independently operated local offices. I live in New York but have visited the ITEX Connecticut trade shows several times. While not as large as some of the local shows, this show offers an opportunity to check out vendors we don't normally do business with. My wife and I also enjoy the drive and ferry ride across the Long Island Sound to get there, fitting in some sightseeing and a meal along the Connecticut shore while we're there enjoying the sport of bargain hunting for a great barter deal.

Your first trade show will also offer you an opportunity to meet the entire office and sales staff, which you probably have only talked to on the phone.

Putting a face to a name and meeting face to face can be helpful in building relationships. Find out who's in charge of what in the exchange office if you don't already know and store that information for future use. Let the people who work for you get to know you and like you, they will work harder for you or pass deals your way more often. Trust me this works to your benefit when done right.

Don't forget when you're shopping, if you run low on funds, the credit manager, who you should now know, can extend you a line of barter credit or increase the amount of credit you already have. This will allow you to make additional purchases and take advantage of deals while maximizing your shopping experience. If you have created a negative balance in your account, you can sell your products or services later to reduce the shortfall. What was that credit manager's name?

Another way to increase your purchasing power at a trade show is to bring along one or more of your staff members that you might give a bonus or perk to for the holidays. Give them a credit line of their own, and let them loose in the aisles to find whatever they would like to buy within their budgets without having to shell out the cash. They get a mini shopping spree experience and you just sign! This works for family too if you want to treat Mom or anyone, this would be a great time to say thanks in an extra way. Barter has certainly allowed me to be more generous in many ways leaving me feeling good about being able to do so. Employee perks are also tax deductible but check with your accountant on how to handle this if it's intended to be extra compensation and not just a gift.

Networking

In addition to being exposed to products and being able to spend as much of your trade dollars as you can on tangible items instead of services, every trade show is a networking event. One of the most important aspects of working a trade show is *working* the trade show like it's a networking event. Bring plenty of business cards and flyers, brochures or other literature if you have it. The exchange usually has a table set up for those who want to market their products or services to other members. You should also be collecting business cards to build your network of traders. A trade show is a great way to meet and speak with local business owners, creating the opportunity to forge relationships and to cross promote your businesses. You can also learn what trade deals and benefits your new friends get from trading. Don't be shy, ask, you never know what you'll learn. What's the best deal they've made? Where do they dine on trade?

Sales Tax

If you live in a state where sales tax is applicable to certain purchases; bring cash, checks or your credit cards to cover what you might have to pay the vendor for in tax. Keep in mind, some vendors may only accept cash as they might not want to take checks or have the ability to process credit cards

at the trade show venue.

ALWAYS
SELL YOURSELF

CHAPTER 8

SELLING AT TRADE SHOWS

At trade shows, as a vendor, you should be selling and while you're there you need to make time to buy as well. The same benefits discussed previously for buyers all apply, plus a few more things outlined here to consider as a seller. Some exchanges charge to exhibit, usually in trade dollars but there could be cash fees as well. When filling out a request for space be sure to think about your special needs and do not assume anything will be available or included within the space. This means everything from tables to table cloths, chairs, electric, lighting, running water etc.

Arriving early to set up is important because you need to see the lay of the land, so to speak, and pick the best location to set up shop. If spaces are pre-assigned, then make sure the spot you have been assigned is in a high traffic location or ask to be moved before other vendors come in and stake claim to the primary selling locations.

What is a primary selling location? Near the main entrance because you catch customers at least twice in the day as they pass you, literally coming and going, compared to vendors in the back of the room who may only be passed once or sometimes missed completely. Some vendors like to be near the food areas where people congregate or the restrooms because they generate traffic. Clothes vendors quickly learn the restrooms double as changing rooms for them and therefore exponentially increase their sales because of the customer comfort level and convenience the restrooms offer compared to trying on clothes behind a makeshift curtain.

Vendors selling large and cumbersome or very heavy objects such as statuary and artwork often prefer to be close to the loading area to reduce setup and breakdown time. This can greatly reduce physical effort and handling damages. Even though I know the space near the entrance usually has more traffic, as a jeweler, security and other needs make being against a wall a plus for me. I can have easy access to electric outlets for lighting and I don't have to worry about anyone behind me or customers cutting through booths adjacent to me. The security and comfort of a wall allows me to focus my attention in one direction towards the front of my counters. Vendors develop their own favorite spots if the same venue is used every year for a multitude of reasons.

The next consideration when selecting a selling space is whether to pick a corner or straight space. Corner booths always provide more traffic because customers pass multiple times in different directions. Corner locations also allow for more table frontage than a single booth, but are harder to work for many vendors such as myself. I prefer to work with a straight line of showcases. I usually take two adjacent booths and align my showcases in a row rather than trying to negotiate the tight quarters of a corner booth that also creates potential security issues for me.

On the surface a trade show is a place to buy and sell, but it's also an opportunity to do a little shameless self-promotion. Always sell yourself.

Bring plenty of business cards and flyers, placing them where members can pick them up without having to ask for one. Trade shows can get very busy at times and people will just pass you by if they feel you're too busy to interrupt. Many customers will also not ask for prices, for this reason some signage and easy to read price tags will help improve sales and help shoppers identify bargains. This will also translate into your customers being able to help themselves; resulting in more sales and/or larger sales per transaction.

As a jeweler, I like to attend trade shows to sell just before the holiday season when the demand for jewelry is highest because I can build up my trade credits substantially in one day. This is better for me than working one on one with customers by appointments in my stores, which can become very time consuming. In the store a customer might spend five minutes or two hours to make a two hundred dollar purchase, while at a show I would do twenty thousand to forty thousand dollars of business within an eight hour day. I also move out many low priced items suitable for gifts, which fits my business plan better than trading very big tickets with high replacement costs. It's simply much more efficient for me to sell this way.

I bring all of the items I am willing to trade or need to remove from my inventory to shows and sell them at full retail instead of having to create a sale section in my store which my top salespeople hate. Salespeople want to sell what's new and cool, not what's been in the store a few months or worse, a few years. Sometimes inventory ages by default when you experiment with new products that just don't sell in your market or you miscalculate the amount you purchase in relation to actual sales results. This doesn't mean there's anything wrong with these products, but they need to find a home. As my wife likes to say; "We are operating a business here not a museum!" She also likes to say; "We can't afford to keep inventory that has lots of birthdays in our store."

For many retailers who experience inventory challenges, a trade show offers the forum to readjust and capitalize on stale dollars stifling ones potential.

This is the chance to clean out your stock room, move stale inventory and eliminate duplicates. You can even sell off your seconds or slightly damaged items as long as you identify them as such to be fair. You no longer have to remain a victim of aging product, fashion blips, and styles that are changing or your customers have no interest in.

I have a lot of "one of a kind" estate and antique jewelry items in my stores that are valuable, but difficult to sell because they are unique. A trade show gives me new chances to showcase these unique items and sell to customers that have not been exposed to my inventory and may have different tastes than the people who shop at my stores.

Usually trade exchanges don't impose any limits on what you can sell, outside of illegal items or if they have offered a vendor an exclusive for some reason. Therefore, some merchants use this as an opportunity to host their own little *garage sale* and they bring some new or used personal items to sell in addition to their normal products. Look around your basement and garage and even your business storage areas to find something you're not using that might better serve you if converted into barter credits. Have an old or extra copy machine, fax machine or furniture in the office you don't use any more? I can pretty much guarantee you this; you won't be taking home office equipment if you bring it to a trade show to sell. There's always a buyer for used business equipment and a myriad of other things, just use your imagination.

One of the reasons sellers at trade shows do so well is that buyers are eager to buy, they want to find value for the trade dollars they have accumulated in their accounts and when they do, they are highly incentivized to continue to trade more often and for larger dollars. When shopping a November or December trade show I am also keenly aware that as the end of the year approaches, the time left to find tax deductions wanes as well. I'm happy for the opportunity to buy extra supplies and things I might need in the future to take advantage of extra tax savings in the current year.

These reasons coupled with the group dynamics of a trade show when it gets crowded can create buying frenzies that you benefit from as a seller. Some vendors sell so many products they bring more than one vehicle or use their truck to store extra stock. At one show they had a vendor who brought a truck full of stereo speaker sets and he was just selling them off the back of the truck at the entrance to the show rather than trying to bring them inside where he only set up samples for people to see.

Creative Selling

One member who owned an art gallery made a deal with his exchange to host an auction at a trade show. He brought all kinds of interesting artwork he wanted to move out of his inventory and the exchange provided him with a forum and patrons to bid on his offerings. What a great and creative way to capitalize on a captive audience! There was quite a crowd and he seemed to do very well. I still enjoy the framed Leroy Neiman "America's Cup" depicting the 19th Challenge Newport Sailing event, which I was the successful bidder on. Think about what opportunities you might create for yourself in a trade show environment within your space or by working with the exchange.

Be prepared to promote yourself, some shows make regular announcements of special offers at specific booths, or employ other tactics to highlight vendors or products. Have a really great idea or promotion? Talk with your broker or exchange manager about placing an easel at the entrance or displaying a sample at the check in table with your booth number on it.

Be Prepared for Cash Transactions

As a vendor at trade shows I have also had the opportunity to make some cash transactions as well. Sometimes the staff at a venue will ask if they can purchase an item and obviously they don't have barter credits. I've also had employees of members shopping who have been given a dollar limit to spend; who are willing to pay the difference in cash for something they've wanted to buy that is more expensive than the budget they received. Employees of sellers working the show may also make cash purchases and even members who might be closing out their account and have used their remaining credits will pay some cash, so always be prepared for the opportunity to take real cash at a trade show.

Sales Tax

If you are in a state that requires you to collect sales tax, be prepared; have sufficient change on hand so you are not one of those vendors asking everyone for change every time you make a sale, it's distracting from your purpose of being there. We accept credit cards for those cash sale opportunities that arise, to collect sales tax and for when customers spend more than they expected, finding themselves short of cash. In New York, if we sell a five thousand dollar bracelet with an 8.625% sales tax rate, the customer has to pay $431.25 in cash for the tax and may not have been prepared to do that, especially if they have already done a lot of shopping. We try

to make it easy for our customers to buy from us by accepting

many forms of payment.

DARE
TO GO IT
ALONE?

CHAPTER 9

WHAT IF I DON'T WANT TO USE
A BARTER EXCHANGE?

The world is full of barter opportunities if you don't want to use an exchange, but I will tell you it is infinitely easier to use an exchange to locate trading partners and facilitate trades than going it alone. This section will likely expose more negatives related to direct trading than positives as for each benefit I mention, there are caveats that make these options difficult or uncomfortable for many people to follow through in developing trading relationships. You can and should do business both ways, just understand the advantages and disadvantages of each first.

When companies and individuals barter or trade with each other; without using a trade exchange, it is referred to as a *Direct Trade*. The significant advantage in a direct trade is saving the fees that you might pay, but you will forfeit many of the benefits exchanges offer. You save the typical ten percent transaction fees, plus other costs exchanges impose, which can add up to a lot of money over time. You do however have risks in trading with people you have never done business with before that exchanges mitigate as part of the services they offer, validating the fees they charge.

Direct trades can offer the benefit of privacy, or in some cases anonymity, if you don't exchange personal information in a direct trade with someone. There are reasons this would appeal to some, but in most above board transactions this is not a significant consideration. While you do lose some sense of privacy dealing with exchanges, it is not much different than the risks associated with protecting your privacy when using a credit card in the normal course of doing business.

Finding a Trading Partner

There are three easy ways to find trading partners on your own. You can generate leads from the people you already do business with, make some cold calls or get connected online. For the most part options one and two require good networking skills and the ability to accept rejection. If you are outgoing this will be easy, but if you are an introvert you will find this challenging. Getting connected online, although more impersonal, exposes you to thousands of opportunities with people already open to the idea of trading with you and eliminates the stress some people find in the need to do networking.

Unexpected Benefit of Direct Trade

In many instances an unexpected benefit and hidden value of a direct trade is the better service that you receive than cash customers do when you establish a relationship with the owner of a business and deal direct. The ability to bypass receptionists and gatekeepers of all sorts allows you to reap the benefits of human influence. I know this might sound counterintuitive, but it happens all the time because the personal relationship you created has more enduring value than any sale. Some of the contacts I've made with people I met by trading with have turned into long lasting friendships spanning more than a decade. This can of course also apply to relationships created through exchanges.

Generating Leads from Your Customers

In some service industries the nature of your service calls will tell you what business your clients are in, making it easier to identify prospects you would like to trade with. Otherwise you should employ some tact when approaching your customers to strike up a conversation and look for opportunities in any conversation to propose a mutually beneficial trade.

Keep in mind some customers prefer anonymity, they visit your business to accomplish something they need to and may not be interested in discussing where they work or what they do for a living. The last thing you want to do is alienate an existing customer. That being said, when it comes to a business proposition, your customer may be willing to open up.

Allow people that you do make connections with to help you build a network by asking them for referrals of people they trade with, you may be able to barter related services in this manner. Tell people what you are seeking to trade for and let them suggest or cultivate leads for you.

Cold Calls

Just the words *cold calls* give some people the chills. Nothing to fear here, and while this can be done by phone it is much more effective when done in person. The best way to start a cold call is to introduce yourself and let your prospect know what you do, then ask them if they have ever visited your place of business. For this purpose, hopefully they have not, because you are looking for a new relationship: but if they have, then take this moment to thank them. The next step, regardless of their response, is to follow up by asking if they would be interested in doing business with you in exchange for their services. Calling ahead to be sure the owner or person you wish to speak with will be available when you visit might save you considerable time.

Use Your Own Web Site

If you have your own web site, then you can use it to trade your products or services, making them available to barter with others around the country in much the same way you would make them available to members of a trade exchange.

Get Connected to Find Trading Partners

When I started trading, there was no internet. Did I just say that? It's true and the ability to research exchanges, trading partners, competitive pricing and gather information about a company or product has never been easier. In the last decade it's become infinitely easier to connect with other traders because of the internet. All kinds of sites have popped up trying to connect buyers and sellers, sometimes for free and sometimes for a fee.

Craigslist and Other Online Sites

Sites like Craigslist have a barter section where you can post an ad stating what you have to offer and what you would like in return. The words of caution here are *Buyer and Seller Beware* as you never know who you might be dealing with online. Always insure your personal safety first. Unfortunately there are documented tragedies that have occurred which began with online transactions that went wrong.

When you visit *https://www.craigslist.org/about/sites#US* you can drill down to your local state then closest city or towns listed, and then select the barter section. Here you will find others looking to trade everything from used household items to new products.

Phone Apps

There are now a myriad of *Phone Apps* available for the trader who is always on the go. Mobile is no longer just a tool to use when you are out of the office; it has replaced the office for many entrepreneurs. A simple search of "Barter" in Google Apps will provide you with options that are sure to be of interest. While I am not endorsing the site I am about to mention, I would like to use it as an example of the diverse offerings available online and invite you to rethink how you can implement changes in the way you manage your lifestyle and your business. *Barter Babies* has an App which is self-described as follows: "Barter Babies is an online network that allows parents from all over the United States to connect with other parents in their local area to exchange childcare for free". This may sound like a personal service, but it is relevant to the business world in the respect that childcare can impact your ability to get to work on time or more often. This may be the type of service that would assist your staff as well so if you have a barter need there's probably an App for that!

Keep Accurate Records

When conducting direct trades you must do the record keeping; so establish a manner in which you record your

transactions that you can pass on to your accountant at tax time.

If you are going to have open balances with trading partners, supply them with statements from time to time to confirm balances due and avoid disagreements. Save receipts and invoices for everything you buy and sell. Save your trade exchange statements for seven years in case you need to produce them for an income tax or sales tax audit that might occur during the normal course of business.

The Primary Negative of Direct Trade

The primary negative of direct trading is that you have to find people who have what you need and are willing to trade for what you sell in an amount equal to what you are willing to spend. This can consume considerable time and energy often resulting in the inability to find what you are looking for. When you locate a potential trading partner, you then have to agree to the fair value in a trade as opposed to exchange transactions where the value of a trade dollar is the exchange rate.

Unlike direct trades, exchanges allow you to sell when you want to and buy when you want to without having to be concerned about the other side of the transaction to make a deal. If your business is servicing cesspools, then it doesn't matter if the florist wants or needs your services when you buy flowers because you are exchanging a credit and don't have to provide the florist with anything else, just charge the purchase to your account.

The layer of recourse an exchange offers is also missing. If you run into serious problems negotiating your deal, you'll probably end up in court or have to write off some bad debt, much the same way you would if a cash transaction were to go bad. An exchange can almost always prevent that from happening.

ALL THINGS BEING EQUAL... THERE'S NO EQUALITY

CHAPTER 10

IS A BARTER DOLLAR EQUAL TO A CASH DOLLAR?

Is a barter dollar equal to a cash dollar is a question I'm often asked by people who know I barter a lot and are interested in learning more. The answer is yes and no. The IRS and State governments value barter or trade dollars as U.S. currency, making them equal to cash dollars, making no distinction for the purposes of accounting and filing tax and information returns. So the answer is yes under this definition and clearly barter dollars are real dollars and equal in value to cash dollars.

So why then will you hear people refer to trade dollars as "*Monopoly Money*" and say they are not equal to cash dollars? The answer can be found in the buying power of barter dollars not the accounting value of them. In reality, the value you receive for each dollar you barter can be different in a positive or negative way. The goal is to always barter for at least "*Fair Trade*" for your barter dollars making them equal to cash. This can be accomplished by understanding how to unlock the value in trade credits and not become jaded by those who do not understand how to maximize the value of theirs.

Fair Trade

Fair trade occurs when you get the equivalent of a cash dollar for your trade dollar in a transaction. When you dine in a restaurant and select items off a menu with prices that are not flexible and then use your barter credits instead of paying cash to settle your bill, you are exchanging those credits dollar for dollar in value. This is an example of the ideal situation, and how the system is designed to work. You will run into members who have learned to take advantage of the system through leverage, while others just charge more for the same goods and services they offer their cash customers.

When the face value of a sporting event ticket is bartered for the same price, it is a fair trade transaction. Although those tickets may be subjected to discounts if they remain unsold for cash in the final days or hours prior to the event, they are rarely discounted when traded and their face value is still considered their fair market value when sold. As we know, tickets for concerts, sporting events and other types of entertainment can often sell well above their face value, therefore just because something has a premium attached to it doesn't automatically mean it is overpriced in the market place.

Businesses that do not have price tags, posted pricing such as a menu or a price list that you can reference to compare value, make it more difficult for you to ascertain what value you will be receiving when making a trade. Beware of businesses that up charge because you want to barter with them. Although unfortunate, I have encountered up charging, and other traders have shared many stories with me of their experiences with *"up charging"*; commonly with people in the construction trades, where they will quote a cash price and a trade price for the same work.

In all fairness, not to bash the construction trade as an industry, I have also received quotes from barter members that were much lower than cash estimates from other contractors, so the lesson is to always get several quotes on any significant barter purchase or home improvement you are planning. Compare apples to apples as best as you can. For these purchases you should know if you are getting the right value; don't just feel you're paying too much. You may find you really had no idea of what the job should cost in the marketplace, which is why you should always get several estimates on large projects. Construction estimates seem to come in much higher than people expect because there are many hidden costs that are overlooked by a homeowner, which a professional will see and take into account when preparing an estimate for you.

If you come across a member that tries to severely overcharge, then you should report them to your exchange so appropriate action can be taken to protect all members.

Use Barter Dollars First

Always try to use your barter dollars first; it's a lifestyle change that's well worth making in the long run.

If you find you can accumulate trade dollars easily as I do, then you will conserve a lot of cash as you replace it with bartering because it doesn't diminish your cash inflows. Always find the highest and best use for your cash and trade dollars by establishing a natural pecking order of purchasing with trade dollars, a blend of trade dollars and cash or just cash when necessary that becomes a part of the way you think about everything you buy.

New Members

Unfortunately, I think some exchanges do a disservice to new members by not encouraging them to walk before they run. I believe these exchanges should have new members make purchases before they sell, encouraging them to think about their goals and set limits while they become familiar with the system. There is a conflict of interest for an exchange which makes its money by encouraging members to sell as much as they can because they are motivated by the commissions they will earn. Exchanges need to balance the value of the customer against the value of a sale while watching out for the well-being of the new member. Remember the exchange gets a commission in every transaction even if the new member isn't paying it at the time of a transaction. As a result, new members are often thrown to the wolves.

New members not only offer products that may not have been available in an exchange, but they also tend to be less limiting in the dollar value of transactions, items they could sell for cash and orders that will result in cash outlays which is a pitfall for them, but it's an advantage for members with pent up spending needs. The reality is you will often benefit if you visit new members early, before they might have the opportunity to become overwhelmed or disenchanted.

Is Currency of Exchanges Interchangeable?

Generally, the currencies of exchanges are not interchangeable for you as a member of an exchange. Yet some exchanges do belong to other master trade exchanges of barter companies on a wholesale level if you will, or they have reciprocal agreements with other exchanges. You could think of this as trading on a wholesale level, where an exchange becomes a middleman between a third party and you. This allows your exchange to trade with other exchanges to obtain items you may need, or provide additional avenues for you to sell your products or services as well. The exchange handles the interchange of credits for you on their books. Your transaction through a third party will probably show up as a debit or credit with your exchanges office on your monthly statement.

Are All Trade Exchange Dollars Equal?

In a manner similar to foreign currency exchange rates, the value of a dollar from one exchange is not always equal to a dollar in value from another exchange. Even though as previously noted, the IRS values them equally. Or at least this is true in the minds of many traders even though exchanges may value their currencies equally. What values or devalues a trade exchanges *currency* if you will, is determined by a variety of factors that impact traders. Factors affecting value are different for each individual but would include the size of the exchanges membership and the ability to spend the exchanges dollars readily and for fair value.

The Tipping Factor

Out of pocket dollars in a trade are defined as your actual cash cost of your trade dollars plus any cash you add to a deal plus any fees you might have to pay an exchange to complete a deal. Based on your markup or profit margins, you should be able to determine your *tipping factor* or breakeven point, where trade transactions actually cost you the same out of pocket dollars as a cash transaction would. The closer you come to your tipping point the less leverage you are getting on your real cash in your trade transactions.

While it still might be worth doing a transaction that is close to or even equal to your tipping point, focusing on improving the distance between the cash value of a transaction compared to the out of pocket cash dollars you are spending to make a trade should be monitored.

BARTER CREDITS DON'T ADD UP, THEY MULTIPLY THROUGH LEVERIDGE

CHAPTER 11

UNDERSTANDING THE MATH

Although there are examples in several chapters outlining the power of leveraging dollars through barter, I think the importance of understanding the math behind the science is a concept that warrants a chapter devoted solely to the subject. This chapter should also serve as a reference from time to time.

I know a lot of people hate math, but understanding the power hidden in numbers will help you make infinitely better deals. Everyone from a retiree opening a small shop to keep busy, to someone who runs a multimillion dollar enterprise, has had different levels of exposure to the concept of barter; so I will start with the basics of business math.

Gross Profit Margin is the actual amount of money that you make, your profit, on an item without adjusting for any selling expenses. It is a simple calculation, arrived at by deducting

the cost of an item from its selling price.

Gross Profit Margin:
$125 Selling Price – $100 Cost = $25.00 Gross profit

Markup is <u>how much you add to the cost of an item</u> you buy

to resell. Mathematically, it is the percentage difference

between your actual cost and selling price. If your product

costs one hundred dollars, the selling price with a 25%

markup would be one hundred and twenty five dollars. Here

are some examples:

Markup = Cost times a percentage of cost
to determine retail price

25% Markup: $100 Cost x 25%

Math is: $25.00 Profit + $100 Cost = $125 Retail

Or 1.25 x $100 Cost = $125 Retail

50% Markup: $100 Cost x 50%

Math is: $50.00 Profit + $100 Cost = $150 Retail

Or 1.5 x $100 Cost = $150 Retail

100% Markup: $100 Cost x 100%

Math is: $100.00 Profit + $100 Cost = $200 Retail

Or: 2 x $100 Cost = $200 Retail

200% Markup: $100 Cost x 200%

Math is: $200.00 Profit + $100 Cost = $300 Retail

Or: 3 x $100 Cost = $300 Retail

Markup Percentage is the <u>percentage of profit</u> you add to your cost. If you buy something for one hundred dollars and sell it for one hundred and twenty five dollars your profit is twenty five dollars. The twenty five dollars profit is then divided by the retail price of one hundred and twenty five dollars to arrive at the markup percentage. Here are some more examples:

Markup Percentage =

Gross Profit divided by your Retail Price

$25 Profit on $125 retail sale = $25 Divided by $125 = 20%

$50 Profit on $150 retail sale = $50 Divided by $150 = 33.3%

$200 Profit on $300 retail sale=$200 Divided by $300=66.6%

Please note in the examples of Markup and Markup Percentage how the numbers differ. Many people confuse these terms believing a 25% Markup is the same thing as 25% Markup Percentage, which you can now clearly see is not the same thing. Here is the difference:

25% Markup yields a 20% Markup Percentage

50% Markup yields a 33.3% Markup Percentage

100% Markup yields a 50% Markup Percentage

200% Markup yields a 66.6% Markup Percentage

Applying the Math

Understanding your markups and profit margins from a percentage perspective will help you evaluate the value you receive for your trade dollars when you spend them. It will also allow you to calculate the impact your bartering will have on your profit and loss statement if you monitor this periodically. With a comprehension of the percentages, applying the math will allow you to make informed decisions that may on the surface appear to be contrary to traditional thought processes. However, understanding what products or services will actually cost you with leverage will help you make trades you might otherwise not consider to be worthwhile.

Leveraging Your Trade Dollars

If you needed to replace the roof on your home or business, conventional wisdom would tell you to get at least three estimates for a significant expense to compare costs and learn more about the task you are under taking. Each estimator will often look at the job from a different perspective which is not always what is in alignment with the customer's thought process, such as the cheapest way out or best quality roof or best warranty etc.

After getting the estimates, price alone is not always the deciding factor, especially if you are going to barter the job. So let's say your cash estimates are $5,500, $6,000 and $7,900. After comparing you decide to go with the contractor in the middle, even though he wants a little more money than the low man, you like him better and he seems to really know his business. So $6,000 is your cash cost to replace the roof and it is exempt from sales tax because it is a capital improvement to your property.

Now you call in a barter member to give you an estimate. The new estimate comes in at $10,000. Wow, he is expensive! Ten grand for a six thousand dollar job, he's over priced by four thousand dollars or sixty six percent ($4,000 overage divided by $6,000 cash cost). If the barter price is $10,000 compared to $6,000 cash which would you choose? $6,000 I suspect if you determine the estimates are similar, especially if you're trying to get fair value for your barter dollars you would go with the cash quote, but wait…

At this point people that barter often get frustrated, and in many instances rightfully so because they feel they can't use their hard earned trade credits to get what they want at a fair price. They might even be wondering why they joined a barter exchange. But for some people that trade based on the math of a trade, this deal cannot only work, it may put money in their pockets or at least reduce their actual cash expenditures when the math is said and done. This is what happens with the leverage of your purchasing power through barter. Your leverage has to do with your profit margins and the cost of the goods you sell. Here is how the numbers in the deal work:

If Your Cost of Goods is = 33.3%

For the purposes of this exercise we will assume you pay a10% commission to your trade exchange. If your cost of goods or services when selling is one third of your selling prices, then your actual cash cost of ten thousand dollars in barter credits will be 33.3% of $10,000 which is $3,333.33 and here is the math.

Example 1:   33.3% Cost of Goods
$3,333 = Cost of goods or services to acquire trade dollars
    (33.3% of $10,000)
$1,000 = Commission to exchange (10% of $10,000)
$4,333 = Total actual cash cost

Now compare this to the cash quote:

$6,000 = Cash price

-$4,433 = Total actual cash cost

$1,567 = Cash available for other uses

Your actual cost for the job through barter is also only 74% of the original cash quote, calculated as $4,333 divided by $6,000. Even though the barter price started out 66% higher than your cash quote! This is good leverage in your favor, saving you $1,567 in actual cash PLUS you are using the $3,333 in previously paid product costs, which was a non cash conversion of your time or assets into trade dollars. Because your cost of goods is an asset converted to trade credits, it's not really cash even though you paid to acquire these assets at some time in the past. Therefore, you effectively only paid out the $1,000 commission in hard money from your current cash flow or just under 17% of the original cash quote leaving you with a net of $5,000 in real dollars that you would have needed to pay the cash contractor. You now have the remaining $5,000 to do something else with. You may want

to read this paragraph again☺.

If Your Cost of Goods is = 20%

Let's look at what happens to a business with higher profit

margins than the sixty six percent I used in the example

above. Higher margins equal lower cost of goods as shown in

the example below where profit margins are 80% and cost of

goods are 20%.

Example 2:   20% Cost of Goods
$2,000 = Cost of goods or services to acquire trade dollars
   (20% of $10,000)
$1,000 = Commission to exchange (10% of 10,000)
$3,000 = Total actual cash cost

      Now compare this to the cash quote:
$6,000 = Cash price
-$3,000 = Total actual cash cost
$3,000 = Cash available for other uses

Your actual cash cost for the job is now just 50% of the

original cash quote calculated as $3,000 divided by $6,000!

This is awesome leverage in your favor, saving you $3,000 in

actual cash PLUS you are using the $2,000 in previously paid product costs, which was a non cash conversion of your time or assets into trade dollars. So you still only payout the same $1,000 commission from your current cash flows leaving you with the same net of $5,000 to do something else with. Your actual cash position hasn't changed in this scenario, but your purchasing power or available cash has almost doubled from $1,567 to $3,000! This is a great deal and a win-win by any standard.

If Your Cost of Goods is = 0%

Now let's look at what happens for those who trade their time and experience without a hard dollar cost to acquire trade credits. These businesses and professionals have a 100% profit margin and no cost of goods.

Example 3: 0% Cost of Goods
$0.000 = Cost of goods or services to acquire trade dollars (0% of $10,000)
$1,000 = Commission to exchange (10% of $10,000)
$1,000 = Total actual cash cost

Now compare this to the cash quote:
$6,000 = Cash price
-$1,000 = Total actual cash cost
$5,000 = Cash available for other uses

Your actual cash cost for the job is now just under 17% of the original cash quote calculated as $1,000 divided by $6,000! This is awesome leverage in your favor, saving you $5,000 in actual cash to do something else with. Your actual cash position hasn't changed in this scenario, but your purchasing power has gone up to 83%! In this scenario your trade dollars are almost as good as cash but the true value is in what you received for bartering your down time. This is a deal that can only be beat by renegotiating your commission rate, yes I am relentless and you might want to read this paragraph again too.

If Your Cost of Goods is = 50%

Now let's look at what happens to a business with lower profit margins than the 66.6% I used in the original example. Here we reverse the math using lower margins which equal higher cost of goods as shown in this example where profit margins are 50% and cost of goods are 50%.

Example 4: 50% Cost of Goods

$5,000 = Cost of goods or services to acquire trade dollars
   (50% of $10,000)

$1,000 = Commission to exchange (10% of $10,000)

$6,000 = Total actual cash cost

Now compare this to the cash quote:

 $6,000 = Cash price

-$6000 = Total actual cash cost

 $0.000 = Cash available for other uses

This looks like it's not a good deal, BUT...I used this

example because it demonstrates the breakeven point or

tipping point where actual cash in a transaction equals actual

cash out of pocket expense to complete a trade in assets and

cash. In this scenario, even though the sales price of the roof

was inflated by sixty six percent, you have to ask yourself if

you would rather trade $5,000 in old inventory or non-cash

assets plus $1,000 cash instead of coming up with the full

$6,000 in hard money from current cash flow or your bank

account to make this purchase.

Bear in mind that sometimes you might not ever be able to

convert the assets you're trading into the cash equivalent we used, or would have to mark them down to anywhere from fifty cents to ten cents on the dollar. If that's true then the trade is a good deal. If the assets you are trading have high value or need to be replaced when sold then it would not be a good deal and so you have arrived at the tipping point. This is why some members justify paying more than retail with "Monopoly Money".

In this situation of inflated pricing, if you're working on less than 50% gross profit margins, then bartering can become too expensive. I would consider this a poor use of assets and overpriced for you because the math no longer works in your favor.

If your business has large gross margins, can you imagine the amount of leverage you could attain against fair pricing? Obviously a barter price that would be closer to the cash price would reduce the commission costs and your cost of goods in all examples, thereby increasing the leverage tremendously for all examples. I used these scenarios to show that barter pricing alone, when compared to cash pricing, cannot be the determining factor as to whether or not it's worth it to make a deal.

Fair Trade

Here's the same example of the roof at $6,000 trade compared to $6,000 cash with a 20% cost of goods and 80% profit.

Example 5: 20% Cost of Goods

$1,200 = Cost of goods or services to acquire trade dollars
   (20% of $6,000)
$ 600 = Commission to exchange (10% of $6,000)
$1,800 = Total actual cash cost

Now compare this to the cash quote:
$6,000 = Cash price
-$1,800 = Total actual cash cost
$4,200 = Cash available for other uses

Your actual cost for the job is now only 30% of the original cash quote calculated as $1,800 divided by $6,000! This is how leverage works in your favor.

Understanding your margins and your cost of trade dollars will allow you to use these formulas to calculate the exact leverage you will achieve. After a while you'll just know what the percentages of your hard costs are by simply calculating your cost of goods, adding a commission and dividing it by the selling price in your head.

If you only use your dollars to conduct fair trade purchases where inflated prices don't erode your purchasing power, then you can make transactions work with smaller profit margins.

There is an inherent multiplier in the value of your leverage if you accrue barter dollars with leverage and spend them with leverage in the opposite direction.

Barter dollars are much easier to accumulate than cash dollars. I could probably barter a few million dollars a year but I couldn't realistically spend it on enough expenses in relation to my overall cash business. I also wouldn't want to be in a position where I needed to come up with the cash to restock that inventory I bartered so I could maintain my cash business. Therefore what might happen if you oversell, which has happened to me, is that you would accrue too many credits in your trade exchange account for your foreseeable needs.

If you had $6,000 in cash at the bank prior to doing the roof, you would have the following balances in your account after having the roof done under the choices described: In a cash transaction you would have a $0.00 balance – your cash would be gone!

In examples #1 through 4 you would have a $5,000 balance

In example #5 you would have a $5,400 balance

The kicker here is; if the roof or any other expense is for your business, then the full ten thousand dollars in barter paid for the job would be tax deductible. This means the government will subsidize the cost of the repair in an amount determined by your tax bracket. Imagine if you are in a fifty percent tax bracket? Your tax burden would be reduced by five thousand dollars – can you say free money?

The Reverse Is True

As I have already said many times, you should barter to conserve cash, but the reverse is true sometimes. It might be well worth it to spend some cash to make a great barter deal.

By allowing the reverse of creating leverage for yourself to happen, you allow a seller to increase their leverage significantly by adding cash to the deal, while providing you with an opportunity that is too good to pass up.

The T-Shirt Deal

I was looking for a large quantity of t-shirts to promote my jewelry business and a film that my wife and I were executive producers for. I wanted to order one thousand shirts for my jewelry stores and one thousand for our movie *The Great Fight* which was going to have its worldwide premiere at the Hoboken International Film Festival.

Most of my barter contacts in the promotional products field did not want to handle the quantity I wanted on trade and I was quoted everywhere from five to nine dollars per shirt in cash on a thousand pieces. I called a fellow out in Chicago that a national exchange referred me to. He offered to design and make me a two sided shirt with metallic gold and silver printing and black details on a name brand shirt for the jewelry stores. He was also going to make a two color piece for the film shirts. He said he could do it but there was a caveat. He was looking to raise funds for a charity so he would do a part cash part trade deal. He was trying to raise five thousand dollars. We negotiated a deal for five dollars in trade and one dollar in cash per shirt for an order of five thousand shirts.

The seller said he wanted to use the cash for a charitable cause, otherwise he normally wouldn't make this offer, but timing was playing a role in his decision since the event was approaching. This seller could have had a million shirts in his inventory, or he wanted to recoup some cash, or the shirts could have cost him a dollar apiece and he took his cash out of the deal; whatever the rationale behind his pricing was, it doesn't matter. I felt good about helping him help others. I couldn't have done better in a cash deal either, so rather than spending the cash on two thousand shirts I leveraged my cash with my trade dollars and took the deal for five thousand shirts.

I gave the shirts out for free to customers with a purchase and to anyone who said they'd wear them. We got a lot of goodwill and promotional value for my buck a pop literally and the supply lasted a few years.

BARTER
WILL ALLOW YOU
TO IMPROVE THE LIVES
OF OTHERS

CHAPTER 12

GIFTS AND EMPLOYEE BENEFITS

You are only limited by your imagination and comfort level of generosity when it comes to gift giving. You may now find yourself considering this in a new way. As gifts are often tax deductible and you have a lower net cost when bartering them, the act of giving is now a win, win, win triple play. You might even enjoy being someone's hero by going above and beyond in using your trade dollars to do something nice for them.

Staff Incentives

You will find ways to compensate your staff with prizes you can use for contests or incentives. Holiday gift baskets and hundreds of other festive items will be available for you to barter. An incentive doesn't have to be a product or service, it can be an experience a staff member might not otherwise have. When our staff met a significant sales goal, we would take them to dinner so they could enjoy a night on the town. We have even thrown in limousine service and sent our staff flowers that we traded as well.

Services often available with gift cards or punch cards you can trade for such as car washes, dry cleaning or a few trips to the ice cream parlor may not be extravagant perks, but they will certainly be appreciated not only for their inherent value but just because the thought counts too!

Think about the things your staff could use instead of a cash raise.

Many of these items are the same perks you should be using yourself. You could offer benefits that will save your staff money while providing the same net effect and conserving your cash. In some instances you can even reduce your cash payroll if the benefit you offer is worth it for an employee to receive less cash and more benefits. Perks and services your staff would usually consider being luxuries will be greatly appreciated and can lift morale when presented in the right light. There is a tremendous amount of room for creativity here.

Individual Credit Lines

If you motivate your staff with goals to drive sales then consider offering a larger bonus than you would normally give in cash to your manager or sales people in the form of a trade credit with your exchange when sales goals are reached. You can step up the bonus incrementally if you like when goals are surpassed by significant margins. Your staff can redeem their credits to visit a spa, take in a show or use whatever services the exchange has to offer them.

Exchanges can provide you with individual credit lines set up as sub accounts of your main account and a separate ID card for each of your staff members to keep the accounting simple. Put your staff in direct contact with your broker to make it easier for all parties while taking one more thing off of your *to do* list. You can use the same concept for family members that work with you as a perk or as compensation, depending upon how generous you choose to be.

In many surveys employees rank the opportunity for training and recognition equal to or above money when it comes to reasons they stay in a job. Vacations, holiday gifts, bonuses to say thank you or stimulate growth in areas of your business, gift baskets, gift certificates to restaurants or a salon are just a few of the creative ways you can empower your staff to be better and more satisfied employees.

You can offer a dental plan. Make a deal with a local dentist to give your staff member a credit of up to a specified dollar value with the dentist. Your employee will then work directly with the dentist to schedule their appointments and have whatever work they need done. The dentist will bill your exchange account as work is performed up to the limits you have agreed upon. If a staff member doesn't use the credits, you have still provided them with the peace of mind a dental plan offers. You can have an annual plan or roll over unused credits for future use. Whatever you, the staff member and your dentist agree on will work.

Is it Time to Throw a Party?

Do you ever treat your staff to lunch, host catered events or throw a holiday party? Entertain your customers more often, boost your staffs' morale and make working for or with you more enjoyable. You can trade for on and off premises catering, a venue to host your event or for tents, tables and chairs if you want to do it yourself. Don't forget to order your invitations early if it's going to be a party of epic proportions. Allow time to locate the centerpieces, balloon arches and other items on your wish list so you can trade for them all.

Florists

Every exchange I've ever dealt with has several florists. You can put fresh flowers in your place of business that your staff and customers will enjoy. You can add a splash of color, and a fresh scent, changing with the seasons, while improving the ambiance wherever you like, but the cash counter or reception desk is a great place to start sprucing up. Florists get a fair amount of business from me because my wife gets more flowers than most women. When she's happy, I'm happy. We send flowers to special customers for their birthdays or just to say thanks, decorate the tables at our holiday parties with centerpieces and order upscale arrangements for the inevitable funerals; in all conserving us lots of cash each year.

Gift Certificates

Gift certificates for everything from restaurants to retail outlets are available to offer as perks for your staff. Many members will be happy to supply you with them because gift certificates often mean the issuer will get a new customer that is not a barter member. Hopefully these new customers will add some cash to the value of the certificate or revisit your business to spend cash.

Charities

The lifeblood of a charity is the funds it raises that allow it to accomplish its mission. Charities can be and are members of barter exchanges creating another win-win for your business if you are the generous type. If you aren't the generous type, I hope this section may persuade you to become more so.

You can make a tax deductible donation with your barter dollars to a member charity, receive a tax deduction for your good natured gesture and feel good about it.

The higher the tax bracket you're in, the more Uncle Sam will subsidize your generosity. When making a significant donation, you can ask your exchange to waive the cash fee and if they are feeling charitable as well, they might just do so, making it even sweeter to help those in need.

The silver lining found when working with charities is that you also usually receive some promotional value for your business, and over time become recognized as a good corporate citizen by members of the community that will patronize your business for cash.

The charity benefits because it uses its credits to reduce costs and to buy things they need, or items they can auction at their events to raise cash. Charities host events that you may want to attend to bolster your recognition in the community and as a new member of their donor family your attendance will surely be appreciated.

Selling to Charities

You can sell directly to charities if you're not in a position or mindset to donate. As I just mentioned, charities are looking for items to auction but they also seek to purchase gifts to reward people whom are significant benefactors or possibly volunteers. Charities have expenses that are similar to businesses that bartering can reduce or eliminate allowing them to become more effective at pursuing their mission. More charities are joining exchanges all of the time. If you have a favorite charity and they are not a member of a barter exchange, you might want to expose them to the concept of bartering as an additional source of revenue for them. In doing so, you might also receive a referral bonus, that you could donate back to the charity and complete the circle of generosity.

What Can You Do For Your Customers?

What can you do to incentivize or motivate your customers to come back more often and to tell their friends and neighbors about you?

What sets you apart from your competition?

Bartering for ways to pamper your customers can be the edge that allows you to dare to be different and rethink the way you have looked at wooing new customers and customer retention in the past. Think about holiday gifts and perks that you can give to your top clientele. Just like your employees, a little recognition offered to someone you do a lot of business with or have known for a quite some time can go a long way!

Accounting Note

When compensating employees, there are tax rules that may apply. Be sure to check with your accountant for clarification of these rules so you avoid any heartache that may result from trying to do something good without understanding the ramifications of doing so. Simply giving a bouquet of flowers as a gift or as a perk to an employee might be considered an office expense. If you sent a staff member on an all-expense paid vacation valued that several thousand dollars this would surely be compensation classified differently by your accountant and may have tax ramifications.

WHY
<u>ARE</u>
YOU DOING THIS?

CHAPTER 13

COMPENSATE YOURSELF

This chapter probably should have preceded the previous one if you believe in the old business adage "Pay yourself first". But I also believe it's noble to put others first. It is true that many business people, especially small business people and those venturing into new startups rarely compensate themselves adequately, if at all. The money that comes in is used to fuel growth or to address debt, which unfortunately for many, may be building instead of waning.

The point of bartering is to make more money, which although not in the form of cash, can be used to acquire the same things you would buy if you had the cash.

Therefore you are substituting a cash transaction with a trade transaction, which would have not taken place without your new found barter revenue. In some instances where you make a swap you actually eliminate the step of having to sell something in order to buy something in a second transaction, saving you time while effecting the same result. So use this new revenue to compensate yourself more appropriately. After all; it is your money!

As you develop your barter network and accumulate credits, you will gain insight and access to things you may have not been exposed to before. Aside from all of the benefits barter can bring your business, it can elevate the level of disposable income you have, or create it if you never had spare change before.

Travel

I saw a sign at the front entrance to a travel agency once that said "Just go away!" See the world or sail the seas if you prefer but get out! Everything from junkets to mega vacations can be traded. Go ahead, make others jealous or envious, I'm giving you permission to take a much needed vacation because by now you should have figured out that you can afford to do it by bartering for it. If you haven't had a break in years, which sadly I hear business people say quite often, then whatever the cost, I assure you the experience can be priceless.

I'm a workaholic, but then, even I take long breaks to find balance in my life. My goal is to travel ten times a year and see some of the world. Some years I only get to go seven or so times and I'm really not disappointed when I haven't achieved my goal.

Time and money; the old excuses that you can't make the time or afford the money to get away should no longer apply.

Plan a Getaway

Travel to me has always meant getting on a plane with my wife and heading somewhere to sightsee or seek an adventure, we are always on the go. I view travelling as a chance to do something I'm not exposed to in my normal lifestyle, like a change in climate during our winters, time to enjoy some breathtaking scenery or to experience the remnants of history first hand. When we travel we always return home exhausted and usually need a vacation.

A getaway on the other hand is much different than travel for us in the sense it provides my wife and I with a chance to enjoy a more local experience by jumping in the car and making a short trip. For me that might mean two or three hours, but it can be whatever you define as a road trip. There's less effort packing, less touring the countryside and trying to fit everything you can into each day because you may never return to a travel destination. The big decision everyday was choosing which cool café we wanted to visit for lunch or dinner.

The scenery or climate doesn't necessarily change much on a getaway, but the venue offers a break in our daily routine and provides time for us, that travel usually doesn't. We use our time to sleep late, enjoy each other and relax because the pace is much slower. It's great for our relationship and could do wonders for yours. We can do this on trade because there are many hotels and inns on Long Island and in the New England area that we love to visit.

Recently we bartered a mini mansion in Southampton NY for two weeks instead of having to rent it for several thousand dollars, as this community demands twenty to fifty thousand dollars a month in season for rental properties depending on the home and its proximity to the town and beaches. This multimillion dollar home had many amenities. Additionally, we had the opportunity to entertain some guests, who also didn't have to travel too far to join us for a few days. We spent some time visiting many of the local tourist attractions, farms, wineries and shops. When we make these getaways instead of day trips, they are much more enjoyable. Day trips are fun in a different way, but for us they always ended up being long tiring outings, culminating with an evening in bumper to bumper traffic for several hours when returning home. Instead we sat in the Hamptons by the pool enjoying cocktails courtesy of our trade dollars.

Treat Yourself

As a consumer, I'm very value driven when it comes to personal purchases. I look at the resale value in most things I buy or consider the use I'll get from a purchase over time so I can amortize the cost in my head to justify buying something for myself. Oddly enough I have the opposite approach when it comes to buying something for my wife. I'll impulsively buy something just because I know she will like it. Seeing her smile or bringing her to joyful tears is priceless and this is the value for me. Sound familiar? If so, here's your chance to break out of self-imposed limitations when it comes to treating yourself and others because the leverage you achieve on your trade dollars will allow you to justify buying something extravagant. Just do it!

The fact that you can calculate your actual cash cost will be a small percentage of the price tag on an item, compared to making the same purchase in hard cash currency, makes it much easier to commit to discretionary purchases and step up your lifestyle at the same time. And yet, there are still opportunities to buy things on trade that will have some residual value, retain their value, or even appreciate in value over time.

Examples of these would be used cars that can be bartered that will have a residual value when you're ready to resell them, a Diamond would retain its value if you wanted to trade it in for something later and a well-researched purchase of artwork may appreciate as it ages gracefully.

Pamper Yourself

I really mean treat yourself some more, so I added this heading. Arrive in style at your next event in a limousine, get a massage, a new hairstyle, a manicure and throw in a pedicure while you're at the nail salon, sharpen your wardrobe and take advantage of the many personal services that will become available to you without spending your cash. You will get to know art dealers, furriers, jewelers, dry cleaners, where to dine, buy cases of wine and where to pamper yourself, all in the normal course of your daily routine.

Let People Know You Are Successful

Few things will build your self-esteem faster than a bunch of unsolicited compliments when you put on your "A" game attending a business or social function dressed to the nines! Improve your personal image, with everything from designer eyewear to name brand clothes. Let people know you are successful! Everyone likes to do business with successful individuals. When you reek of success it sends the message that you know what you are doing and that's what draws people to you. Make it happen, become the light they are attracted to, they spend cash.

Let Your Profit Margins Guide You

The greater your profit margins, the more discretionary and disposable income you will be generating when you barter. Just keep the tax consequences in mind to find the right balance between how much you can expense to benefit your business and how much you can withdraw in a non-cash form of compensation for personal gain. It is the value you find within your personal expenses such as vacations and luxury purchases or simply bartering your dry cleaning instead of paying for it that will determine the balance for you.

Remember, even increasing your tax liability by making personal purchases can be a good thing if you are substituting trade dollars for cash dollars. This means if you were going to spend money on a trip and you bartered it instead, then the money would not be deductible in your business but you would receive the same benefit in terms of the actual vacation. Although you might have higher taxes, you have the money you didn't spend in your hand and the net after taxes is still yours, thereby increasing your personal wealth.

When you spend a disproportionate amount of your trade dollars on personal expenses, compared to business expenses, you create phantom income. If you do not offset the non-cash income with barter or other cash tax deductions, you should be aware that your tax burden will likely rise, which as noted above, is not necessarily a bad thing. Phantom income is explained further in chapter sixteen titled *Taxes*.

Grow As an Individual

Make changes in your life that interest you. Aside from taking in the sights when travelling, you could stay at home and take some music lessons. Have you always wanted to learn how to play the piano? Have you ever had a dream where you were rocking away on the bass guitar? I know some of you will like the sound of that. Tutoring and educational services of all kinds can be bartered. Take on a personal trainer, get the physical therapy you need or yoga your way to a healthier lifestyle. Eat better using a nutritionist and visit the dentist to brighten your teeth. You're going to be much happier when you start bartering your way to a healthier, more successful life and more people will see you smile.

A FEW PHOTOS FROM OUR TRADING EXPERIENCES

A trip to Paris, where we bartered a deal with an all-inclusive hotel. The sights were breattaking and the tours we took were educational. This trip was one of the better benefits we enjoyed from trading limited value in our old inventory for priceless memories that will last forever.

My wife and I took a trip to an all-inclusive couples resort in Cancun, Mexico. The meals, cocktails and hotel were bartered for, the view was provided at no additional cost.

Me, relaxing in the pool in Cancun, Mexico.

An original watercolor by Itzak Tarkay

Beauty is in the eye of the beholder but original signed
artwork has your best chance of appreciation or returning real
cash to you if you decide to liquidate assets down the road.

A Rembrandt etching to add to our art collection!

An uncommon self portrait.

I just wanted to own this piece of history.

500 Home Run Hitters when there were only eleven of them!

A fine antique wood piano by Krakauer Brothers bought with trade dollars

The Two Family Rental Income Property
in the Village of Patchogue that I bartered for!

If you can make a trade for an income producing asset like this piece of real estate I bought, it could be the best use of your resources. I bartered the down payment and cost of the renovations, then flipped this property at a great price, locking in a handsome profit AND converting my barter dollars invested back into cash dollars at the same time!

STOP GIVING
OTHER PEOPLE
YOUR MONEY!

CHAPTER 14

REDUCE YOUR OPERATING COSTS

The wonderful thing about reducing operating costs is that it increases your profits. The downside if it's not a voluntary slashing of expenses is that it can become quite painful to live without some of the things that you have become accustomed to that need to be cut from your operating budget. If the quality of your products or services will be negatively impacted by making cuts, this could be an untenable situation. In severe cases the reduction of operating expenses may even impair your ability to create sales or grow your business further. If things are getting out of control or beyond your abilities, then controlling costs can become a burden and a daunting task that will weigh you down and prevent you from running your business in the way you would like to. You may be able to find an independent consulting firm in your area that is willing to barter services that can be more objective and help you achieve your cost cutting goals.

There are creative ways to reduce your operating expenses just beyond the horizon. You need to identify your needs and develop a plan. If you belong to an exchange, then a frank discussion with your broker should lead to some additional opportunities for you to maximize your trading to this end. Whether you are cutting costs to improve profitability or because it's a necessary evil to stay afloat, the ability to actually reduce costs without sacrificing their benefits is just another reason bartering should appeal to you.

Your variable expenses, which are often the greatest, can be reduced or eliminated in many cases by trading. It can be done simply, efficiently and immediately by bartering for the things that you consume on a regular basis in the normal course of doing business. Below there are a few generic ways in which most businesses can reduce their operating expenses, but you need to think about your specific business and industry to find innovative ways to improve your productivity. The need to do this over the years has allowed me to find some cutting edge solutions in my own industry to address challenges.

Maintenance Costs

Whether you have an office, a retail outlet or manufacturing facility, your maintenance costs limit your profitability, but you can mitigate their impact every time you barter to reduce them. If you can replace your copy machine when it breaks down or change your service contract for maintaining it to a company willing to barter, then you can keep that money for yourself or to reduce your bills.

Need some electrical work done or a plumber? Trades trade their services too. Everything from minor repairs to renovations can be traded if you find a willing partner or trade exchange member to take on your project. Even if you can't barter an entire renovation, just trading the labor costs could save you a tidy sum of cash.

Keep your premises clean and inviting by using carpet cleaners, window washers and cleaning services that can be bartered. Your alarm system can be monitored or installed and office supplies of all kinds can be traded. Update your surroundings with new office furniture or install new carpeting when it's available and don't forget to ask your broker for an installer. Have your HVAC serviced regularly and breathe easier too.

Office Supplies and Tools

Seek to trade for your consumable items and office equipment. I've traded for everything from cases of multipurpose copy paper, reams and reams of it, to staplers, to very expensive copy machines and lots of not so glamorous items that add up to a lot of cost savings nonetheless. Small power tools and hand tools seem to be readily available from many sources. Since I have repair shops in my jewelry stores I find lots of cost savings in this area. Bartering for polishing compounds, sandpapers and small tool consumables like files, pliers etc. have saved me thousands of dollars in cash expenditures over the years.

Gifts and Employee Benefits

Gifts and employee benefits are areas where savings and the benefits of productivity can be so significant that they were already addressed in chapter twelve. Employee benefits and perks are usually the first things that companies look to cut when the need to save money arises. This can result in a lot of unhappy workers and can become even worse if they start to migrate to other companies or your competitors. When times are tough the need to inflate morale rather than deflate it is of paramount importance. Every pair of hands is needed to do more with less to improve productivity.

Giving benefits and perks rather than cutting them can do wonders for changing the direction of your company's morale and growth.

Photography and Graphic Design

Many companies sell by mail order or use printed materials such as brochures to enhance their business; and depending on the size of the project, you may be able to trade some or all of the printing costs. If you are paying a photographer or studio to create images for your catalog, exchanges often have professional photographers who can do more than just family portraits, so look into this and try to eliminate these cash expenses. All of the artwork for your marketing materials can also be created by graphic designers always looking to trade their time and experience for exposure.

Review Your Checkbook & Credit Card Bills

I've just listed a few ideas here that have general applications for a broad base of businesses. There are so many diverse industries and there are equally as many ways to translate converting cash expenses into non cash alternatives that accomplish the same thing. Your checkbook and/or credit card statements have all of the expenses you incur listed in one place, review it and discuss options with your broker to convert these expenses into barter opportunities or seek out a trading partner. After exhausting these avenues, create a wish list of ways to reduce your overhead or in some cases to add things you could not have otherwise afforded to improve the way you conduct business.

Think about customer oriented perks and benefits that you could barter that will reduce your operating costs and provide a better experience for your clients.

While your fixed expenses such as utilities are usually nearly impossible to barter, they can be bartered if they are paid for by a third party such as the building owner, or if you are in a situation where you are subletting space on an all-inclusive basis and these costs are included in your lease agreement. Opportunities to barter rents or trade for storage, office space, retail space and the like do arise.

Re-evaluate Your Suppliers

Are you dealing with a supplier or paying for a service that has lots of competitors? If so, I'm guessing one of those competitors might be willing to woo you away from your current supplier if it means trading some goods or services to open a new account with you. This holds true on a personal and professional level. Examples of business services you might seek to change are your accounting or legal services, as accountants and lawyers are readily available through trade exchanges. Suppliers could also include those that sell hard goods or raw materials that you might resell or use in your manufacturing process. While many of your suppliers may not be willing or able to trade with you, the goal is to find out who you are already working with that is willing to trade with you, before you seek to make changes.

The truth is it will be harder to get those in the wholesale side of a business or industry to trade with you because their profit margins are generally much smaller than those of us in the retail trades and they must rely on volume to make a profit, but that is not always true. This certainly doesn't mean your vendors cannot take on some trade accounts. If they are willing to do this, you should be their first customer, so enlighten some of your vendors as to the benefits of trading and start making some deals.

Talk to suppliers that you might have some leverage with to determine if they would be willing to trade some or all of their products or services with you. Inquire to see if they would be willing to join an exchange where you could purchase their products and they could use the credits to acquire things they need that you can't offer. The simple suggestion that you might have to seek a new source if they can't accommodate you might motivate them to work with you in a different manner. Even if they won't trade with you, you may have just opened the door to negotiate for better pricing so they can retain you as a satisfied customer.

Pay Down Debt

When you reduce your cash operating expenses and free up cash, one of the best things you can do with it is reduce your debt. One path would be to reduce the debt that has the highest carrying cost and the other would be to attack credit lines that have revolving balances so the cash you let go remains available to you in case there is a future need. I prefer to keep my options available and pay down revolving debt first, but sometimes a balance of both may be more prudent based on the interest rates you are paying.

If you have significant assets, bartering to convert the stale assets into cash to reduce debt can ultimately result in the elimination of all debt achieved through better asset management.

BARTER
IS ABOUT
GENEREATING
MORE CASH

CHAPTER 15

BRING IN MORE CASH BUSINESS

Some sellers will find they can bring in new barter business very easily through exchanges while others struggle and constantly seek ways to barter more. The ultimate goal however, should be to remain focused on bringing more cash customers to your business.

Effective Trading

To bring in more cash dollars I would traditionally resort to increasing my cash marketing and advertising budgets. The results of additional business received from spending this money are not easily quantified for me because my weekly sales gyrate significantly based on everything from weather to whether or not we sell big tickets in any given time period. For this reason I was always hesitant to grow my marketing budgets for fear of realizing diminishing returns on my investment, tempered by the fact that there are always other needs for the cash. Bartering gives me an edge when accruing trade dollars that I can use for promotional purposes instead of cash.

Advertising

Advertising is one thing that is relatively easy to barter, which combined with printing can make bartering your goods and services very worthwhile. Not only do they reduce your cash marketing and promotional expenditures, they increase your traffic flow and create new cash business. You most likely will find you are willing to increase your existing budgets as you become more entrenched in using barter to grow your business.

Advertising is readily available on trade because there is so much competition in the field that newspapers, radio stations, cable TV stations, magazines, coupon books, direct mailers and others always have unsold space they are willing to barter rather than give it away or use it for additional editorial space that doesn't bring in any revenue. What is their cost for this space? Nada, zip, zero, zilch; because the issue is going to publication with or without your ad.

I am solicited on a weekly basis in my stores from every form of media you can think of. Salespeople trying to sell their products want me to be on the supermarket shopping carts, on the screens at the local gym, in every classified *PennySaver* or *Town Crier* edition, on the village tourist map, in the ferry guide, on place mats, on the back of cash register receipts, in the welcome to the neighborhood mailing, on buses, at the bus stops, in the malls…. and if you haven't skipped to the next paragraph yet, you will have realized they all want me to advertise in far more places than my cash budget would ever allow me to do without bankrupting my company.

So like many other small business owners, I became jaded when advertisers walked in and rarely became interested in their sales pitch. Ever had a sales person you couldn't get to leave? There is a simple way to do this, but now I have a new approach. The old way was to simply say "I don't have the money to pay for the ad" they were trying to sell me and they ran for the door because they figured they could never collect their commission.

The new way is much better and it opens more windows of opportunity. I simply say "Thanks for coming in, just so you know, before you start your presentation, I only barter for my advertising as my cash budget is already spoken for. Would you be interested in bartering with me?" Now one of three things happens; they run for the door, or they either have to check with their boss or I find out they are the boss and are interested in making a deal. If they are interested they probably have some dead space and even if it's not this issue or for this deadline, maybe in the near future, so we strike up a conversation.

Frankly, being in the jewelry business gives me an advantage when I'm offering to barter, because jewelry often appeals to a broader audience than many other items. Having over six thousand items in each store to work with to make a trade doesn't hurt either. The result seems to be exponential when dealing with a saleswoman. Just saying, hey, women like sparkly jewels and that's a good thing. Find the advantages in your business and capitalize on them more often.

Remember, you don't always have to deal directly with the owner, I have made deals where I bartered jewelry with sales reps from a radio station, that the station used for an on air promotion, because it motivated their listeners to participate in the radio stations' contest. Use your imagination.

Get Connected with Online Marketing

As you know, technology is forever changing and employing tech savvy individuals can make the difference between becoming stagnant or evolving continuously to remain relevant in your marketplace. You can now find people through trade exchanges who are willing to barter their services and all kinds of technical skills that can propel your business forward.

Historically in the almost forty years I have been in business, I have seen changes that have moved my business from hand written notes and manual bookkeeping in green ledgers to sophisticated digital forms of communication and accounting analysis that provides a wealth of information with a few keystrokes on my laptop from anywhere in the world. I watch my businesses remotely from video feeds to my computer and phone. I was one of the first people in an outdoor business to employ the then new cellular technology with a bag phone and car phone to authorize credit cards, exponentially increasing my sales. I was happy to pay the one dollar per minute charges and join the 1K club when I received my first one thousand dollar phone bill because it reflected my success while others could not comprehend its value and only could see the expense as justification for not using this new technology. Use the new tools in every form of social media available to you today and get more connected now.

To Be Seen and Heard

As technology continues to grow, being seen and heard online has new meaning every day. It's becoming more challenging to stand out in heavily trafficked online marketplaces as well. How do you get or increase your share of *eyeballs*, which is another term for visits to your page.

Get In the Video Game

Homemade video's and short film applications have allowed businesses to rethink and reposition themselves as experts in markets created by companies like YouTube. If you want to step up your game, you can find professionals to make you great commercials that can be aired without the traditional costs of TV. The right video can go viral and bring you a worldwide audience. Make yourself a leader in your field or the "go to" place for answers to questions that bring inquisitive people seeking solutions to problems or researching your products to your website and doorstep.

What are you providing in web content that is of interest to the consumers you would like to do business with?

SEO

If you want to build a web based business and you're asking yourself what an SEO is, you need to hire someone to do this for you. SEO is not a new corporate position, it's an acronym for Search Engine Optimization and it relates to how people find you on the internet. If you're serious about bringing more visitors to your website you can hire someone well versed in ways to drive traffic to your digital platform or physical location. Like any other trade, there are strong and weak professionals within the ranks of techies so interview a few potential candidates and ask lots of questions. You will learn a lot along the way and hopefully find the most suitable candidate to work with.

Printing

You can trade almost any printing service and save the cash you've been spending or start marketing your business more effectively. If you have one generic business card on your counter that you use, print them on trade, but you can also personalize them for each employee without feeling the extra out of pocket cost. This is a simple perk with a little prestige for your staff that makes their interaction with each of your customers more personal and motivates your staff to give out more cards within the store and much more importantly, on their own outside of work.

Flyers, brochures, bag stuffers and special offers are the items we use to bring back customers by strategically placing them around the store and putting them in every bag with a purchase to generate repeat business.

Bringing customers back is a golden rule of selling.

Also be sure to ask your trading partners and other businesses to cross promote with you. See if they are willing to distribute the marketing materials you just made on trade!

Post Cards

Post cards are another form of printing but I have created this additional heading because we have found the use of post cards to be our most effective form of marketing. The direct mail strategy works because you can reach out to specific customers in a timely manner with whatever budget you have. You can send out a few or a few thousand post cards at a time. While you probably won't be bartering the postage, you can reap large cash rewards with an effective direct mail campaign strategy so be sure to talk to your printer about this.

Promotional Products

You can get your name out there! Everything from personalized hats and other apparel to promotional products that will help you step up your presence and image within your community are available. I had little black zipper pouches made with our logo in gold and a clip attached. I put eighteen golf tees (which you can personalize) and a business card inside them. Depending on the event I might add promotional offers as well. When attending golf outings, with the permission of the event's organizer, which has always been well received, I snap one on the handle of each golfer's bag while the carts are lined up waiting to go. This allows me to reach a predominately male audience that is tougher for me to market to and is a subtle way for me to develop potential engagement ring commitments, which are a significant segment of my business.

I trade for a lot of promotional products that I give to charities that they can use as raffle prizes or to distribute to their supporters, which bear my name and provide two real benefits. Recipients immediately associate me with and recognize me as a fellow supporter of an organization they care about. I also derive the benefit of seeing my hats and shirts about town, putting my name in front of people within close proximity of my business.

We also have a printer make note pads with our letterhead information that we use and leave on the counters so we can encourage customers to take one home. We have a printer who promotes a special package for these pads with limited quantities when he needs credits and he always sells out, so now we know to respond quickly when the offer hits our email inbox. We do this with jars of jewelry cleaner as well. Anytime you can get your name into someone's home that has some staying power you regenerate subliminal exposure and keep your name in front of people who already work with you.

Signs

There are signs and then there are signs. Everything from inexpensive paper signs, to banners, to ornate neon signs can be traded for. Spruce up your storefront or office and hang some inviting signs in your windows or update that swinging shingle to raise awareness about what you do. Awnings will freshen up your curb appeal and can double as signs or a place to add messages identifying services you offer.

Labels

You can have labels printed on trade with your name, logo and/or contact information. Mailing or shipping labels and product labels can reduce your production costs if you manufacture or sell products wholesale in quantities. I use hot stamped gold foil labels with our logo on them to dress up our packaging, gift boxes and merchandise when appropriate.

MAKE YOUR BUSINESS LESS TAXING

CHAPTER 16

TAXES

Barter transactions are treated in the exact same way cash transactions are treated by your accountant for record keeping purposes because the IRS and State governments' have deemed that a barter dollar is equal to a cash dollar for reporting purposes. Therefore, you are required to keep and maintain records of all of your barter transactions in much the same way you would record your other regular business transactions. If you receive substantial income from bartering, you may be required to make estimated tax payments.

Tax Planning

You should do tax planning with your accountant mid-year, late in the third quarter or near year's end. This will allow you to make adjustments to how much you buy on trade (To create deductions) or sell on trade (To increase gross revenue) based on how your cash business is shaping up. Since there is no distinction between cash and trade dollars to the government, it is important to monitor the effect trading has on your income and to avoid surprises at the year's end. While you might enjoy a happy surprise, few people enjoy hearing they have to write a check that is a lot more than they were prepared for.

The benefit of bartering is that you can make a lot more money. If there's a negative, most people would say it's paying more taxes, which clearly should not be a deterrent although some people do allow it to be, as absurd as it may sound.

Remember, you have control over increasing or decreasing your trading activity to suit your lifestyle and to benefit you from a tax standpoint.

This thought process of holding back on selling doesn't really exist on the cash side of your business since you would never think of turning a cash sale down because it might affect your tax situation. You would always take the extra money, wouldn't you?

Depending on whether your accountant is using a cash accounting basis versus an accrual accounting basis for your record keeping, deductions might be declared for the year in which they are paid, not necessarily the year in which they are used. Therefore you might be able to prepay expenses such as advertising with trade dollars instead of cash and receive the same cash tax benefits from non-cash transactions. When done properly, this can result in huge tax savings.

Tax Form 1099-B

At the beginning of the year, but before February twenty eighth, a barter exchange will send you a 1099-B form for the previous calendar or tax year. A 1099-B form lets you know what the exchange has declared as sales made by you for the prior year and a copy is remitted to the IRS. Your accountant will use this form to reconcile what the exchange statements show and what you have reported your sales as when filing your federal income tax return.

Sales and Use Taxes

Currently, there is no federal sales tax; however, if the state or states you do business in have a sales tax, then you could be required to collect that tax for some or all of your transactions. If you are required to remit sales tax, which is due on taxable items whether you collected the tax or not, you will be required to complete a Sales Tax Return. You should already know whether or not your cash business requires you to do this, otherwise you should consult with your accounting professional.

If you do business in a state that assesses a sales tax, you will also need to know what the policies are for items you ship out of state or purchase from out of state. Sometimes tax is due on incoming and/or outgoing merchandise. There is a tax called a *use tax* which is often overlooked and a large source of revenue for governments; in New York it's more formally known as the New York State Sales and Use Tax.

If you reside in New York State and buy something such as a

boat in another state but have not paid New York State Sales Tax on it at the time of purchase and then bring it back into New York State to use; you could owe a *use tax* instead of a sales tax. This is how states prevent people from going over the border to buy large purchases that have lower or no sales tax rates. The tax rates for *Use taxes* in New York equal the sales tax rate so many people believe it's the same thing. Online purchasing is subject to the rules set by the states. *Use taxes* apply to barter and cash transactions in the same way as they apply to cash transactions.

For barter transactions, sales tax is paid separately in cash, because you would now have a cash tax bill due which is generated by non-cash barter transactions that you might not otherwise have the ability to pay. For this reason you should always collect sales tax in cash or by credit card from barter clients and escrow it in an account separate from the one you use as your businesses operating account in the same way it is recommended to handle sales tax from your cash sales.

Remember, sales tax is not your money; you are only collecting it as an agent for the State that requires you to do so. Because you are an agent, States can and do asses serious penalties when you don't remit the money you have collected on their behalf in a timely manner.

Tax Exempt

As a jeweler, if I buy a watch from another jeweler on barter and offer it for sale in my store, then the transaction would be exempt from sales tax because the item was purchased for resale. I would of course owe the sales tax if I bought the watch for a gift or it was for personal use. Be careful not to accept tax exempt certificates from businesses that do not meet the *resale* criteria. Too often we get someone who tries to circumvent the sales tax rules and we don't allow it. This is an important point because we don't want the sales tax liability to pass on to us if audited. Sometimes it's not a black and white decision though, as evidenced in these two situations:

1. Someone who owns an auto repair shop wants to buy a Diamond bracelet for his wife and use their business resale certificate to waive the required sales tax. In this situation it is clearly not okay because the customers' intention is not to resell the Diamond bracelet in their auto repair shop, confirmed by the fact the husband stated it was for his wife.

2. A tougher call would be if a beauty salon owner presents a resale certificate when making the same purchase. Now you need to determine whether the sale is a personal purchase or if it is intended for resale at the beauty salon in order to accept a resale certificate and to waive the collection of tax on behalf of the State. In New York, the purchaser would also be required to complete a "Resale Certificate", which if completed properly and timely should remove the liability from you. In this case you might only be able to rely on the customer's statement because it's commonplace for salons to have boutiques where they sell jewelry or other items. While you are not the tax policeman, you are responsible to make a diligent effort to ascertain that you are properly waiving the

collection of the taxing authorities' money.

If you accept a resale certificate, be sure to keep it with your tax paperwork in case the need to produce it arises. Also fill out the form before delivering the item; it's so much easier than trying to get it after the fact, even though your customer promised to call you with their resale number or mail you the form as soon as they got back to their shop.

Sales Tax Reporting

For sales tax reporting, we use Excel spreadsheets and keep a running total of our sales to calculate the amount we will have to pay for our monthly or quarterly sales tax. The total sales from our barter transactions are then added to our cash sales and entered as one figure on our New York State sales tax return. If any barter sales were exempt from sales tax, such as items purchased by businesses in our industry for resale or items shipped out of state, then these transactions would be handled in the same manner as exempt cash transactions would be handled on our sales tax return.

We provide these worksheet documents to our accountant at the end of the year to factor into our gross sales reported for income tax purposes. The accountant matches our total sales in barter to the totals on the exchanges monthly statements we receive to confirm we have captured all potential income. At the end of the year, our accountant also compares our sales tax returns to our income tax returns, and our sales to the 1099 forms exchanges send us, insuring everything ties out mathematically.

Income Taxes

Income Tax is a much more complicated issue than Sales Tax and a complete discussion is beyond the scope of this book. I've included many ways to help you think about the ways you can reduce your tax liability by making your barter dollars work for you, but please be sure to read my disclaimer at the end of this chapter.

When you file your annual Federal Income Tax return you will add the components of your barter sales and expenses to the calculations. As noted above, your accountant will already have your sales figures, now you need to provide the information on what you did with the barter dollars you received throughout the year.

Expenses require a little more attention to detail as documentation for any items taken as a tax deduction on your annual income tax return may be requested for review by the IRS. Therefore maintaining accurate records as you go along is a good business practice and will eliminate tremendous amounts of stress, time and energy being expended to organize or obtain copies of receipts if you ever find yourself being audited or required to produce this documentation to substantiate your deductions.

ALWAYS keep your receipts for your expenses to document your tax deductions.

We maintain an expense spreadsheet in Excel as well for each trade exchange we do business with that allows us to easily enter transactions in columns titled by type of expense and see the breakdown by category of how we are spending our dollars. This allows you to follow the percentage of your barter income spent on personal items which are not deductible and may translate to higher reportable net income versus expenses that will reduce your net income.

How Barter Tax Accounting Works

Let's assume for a moment that you have a one hundred percent gross profit margin, which might be true for a professional such as an architect who charges for time and experience, and has no significant out of pocket expenses or *no cost for tax purposes* attached to the services required to render a drawing for you.

In the simplest example, excluding the effect of barter exchange commission's, if an architect started the year with no balance in their trade exchange account, then made barter sales billing for their services and spent all of the barter dollars on tax deductible items, the architect would have a zero balance in their exchange's account at the end of the year. The architect's gross expenses would be deducted from their income taxes, washing out any tax liability on the barter income and the architect would owe no taxes. Every dollar of potential income was erased by the same amount of dollars that were expensed.

Regardless of how complicated the other aspects of the architect's income tax liabilities are, if this balance were achieved each year by bartering, the net effect on the tax consequences of the architects bartering would remain the same. For tax purposes the architect has achieved a zero sum gain/loss. However, the architect has benefited greatly from the additional barter revenue that was used to acquire all of the things purchased in the year; thereby reducing demand on the actual cash income received which would have been needed to accomplish this.

Since most businesses don't have a one hundred percent gross profit margin, if the cost of goods is expensed in accounting terms, then a *phantom deduction* is created, having the opposite effect of phantom income discussed earlier.

Phantom Income

It is extremely important to understand a concept my accountant, who doubles as my brother, always reminds me of that he calls *phantom income*. To explain phantom income I'll use an example of an attorney that has traded ten thousand dollars of services for barter credits and the credits are then used to take a ten thousand dollar vacation with the family. In a situation with all other things being equal, examining only the effects of the barter credits coming in and going out, the following would occur: The sale of the services creates ten thousand dollars in new income for the lawyer but at the end of the year there was nothing to offset that in tax deductible expenses since the barter credits were spent on a personal, non-tax deductible vacation. Therefore, a cash income tax liability would be created based on the tax bracket of the lawyer, even though no cash was received in the transaction. Now, imagine if you bartered one hundred thousand dollars with no tax deductible expense to offset your new found income or barter three hundred thousand dollars on trade and spend one hundred thousand of that on personal expense.

This will most likely raise your taxable income, because in either scenario you have added one hundred thousand dollars to your taxable income. The key is to know how to handle this so as not to incur tremendous cash tax burdens.

Of course this will not happen in every case and you can manage this by being aware of it. If the attorney had used the funds to take a business trip, then the business portion of his travel would have been deductible, so a lesson here might be to combine some business with pleasure that you can write off getting there and back on the business and find some time to enjoy yourself while you're there. Even if you can't deduct the entire sum it should be well worth it.

Because this concept is so important to understand, here is a different example to make phantom or non-cash deductions clearer. Let's assume the cost of a widget sold at retail for fifty dollars is fifty percent or twenty five dollars. With all other things being equal, at tax time the retailer would report fifty dollars in sales and have a twenty five dollar taxable income. If the fifty dollars received in barter credits was traded for fifty dollars in tax deductible expenses, then the fifty dollar deduction would be double what the twenty five dollar income is.

This would mean a tax credit would be due to the retailer who actually would report a loss for income tax purposes. In reality, this loss would be applied against other cash income, thereby reducing the taxes owed on that income. This is why you should be bartering stale assets and converting them into credits that you can purchase tax deductible items with. In the sense that inventory or other assets are converted from equity to expense instead of cash, you would have more deductions than income because you are writing off one hundred percent of your sales but only had a profit of fifty percent. From a tax perspective this is the best case scenario as you would now owe less tax.

What you have actually done is converted your cost of goods or cash equity from the stale assets into a tax advantage by plowing it back into your business as expenses, which frees up cash you would normally have to spend to accomplish the same thing. This may be slightly complicated for the novice trader, but understanding this concept and implementing it properly can help you better manage your cash flow.

On the other hand, if you made barter sales but did not spend any of the barter dollars, you would have credits in your exchange's account and all of this credit would be counted as income. From a tax perspective this is usually the worst case scenario as you would now add your gross sales to your gross income and owe more taxes. This is how you create phantom income, money you have made on paper but never actually held in your hand that incurs a tax liability. There is a silver lining here though, now your after tax trade credits have become an asset that can be used in the next tax year(s), which you can spend on tax deductible items, without having to declare additional income against them since you already declared the sales in the previous year, thereby actually reducing your future cash tax bills.

Why would you do this you ask? This is a tactic that can be employed by sophisticated traders who understand their tax planning and can handle income in the current year knowing the tax deductions could be more beneficial in a future year. Some people know they're going to be in different tax brackets for the current and future year(s) so they may benefit from either accelerating or delaying expenses that would provide more significant tax savings against their income. This can also happen when the government changes tax rates or regulations as we have seen in the past, creating an advantage to claiming deductions before or after the changes are implemented. Simply stated, maybe you have more deductions than you need this year and can handle the income without incurring additional tax liability.

Talk to Your Accountant

Phantom income is only one of the reasons we meet with our accountant at the beginning of the third quarter every year to do tax planning. At this meeting we assess our gross sales, which include cash and trade transactions, against our expenses to get a snapshot of what our income and tax liability might look like. For us it's a challenge because the fourth quarter generates a large portion of our annual sales, so we have to make appropriate estimates. If it looks like we have a large profit coming, we might opt to spend down some of our trade balances more aggressively to create write offs. We can do this by purchasing extra supplies, pre-paid postage, prepaying for advertising, printing our Valentine's Day marketing materials early etc. We may supplement these expenses by becoming more aggressive with our cash as well, thereby reducing our projected taxes due.

Businesses that use barter exchanges to increase their ability to trade, often transact hundreds or thousands of dollars in transactions and some do over a hundred thousand dollars a year in trade. Could you handle that? Hopefully you can or will build your sales up to it, because bartering can be a tremendous source of wealth building.

Professional Expenses

As in the example I used above for the architect and have used for other references to businesses and professionals that have no cost of goods, the expression *no cost of goods* may be a misnomer of sorts. Professionals and businesses that trade time and experience often do have many hidden expenses, they may just be less tangible or more difficult to assess to a particular transaction. Many clients might think they only pay professionals for their time, which may be the case, but there can also be lots of behind the scenes expenses that are not reflected on an hourly billing time sheet. Professionals who opt not to pass along or bill expenses to a customer that have accrued in a barter transaction are accumulating tax deductions which they should be writing off at tax time as well.

Other Deductions

All of the fees you pay to exchanges, whether in the form of trade dollars or cash, are tax deductible.

Shipping charges, gratuities and other cash expenses associated with tax deductible expenses that were bartered are also tax deductible. Be sure not to overlook any of these items when preparing your tax returns.

Other Taxes

When bartering, beware that there may be other tax liabilities you can become responsible for. Every state regulates business in a different way. Pennsylvania for example has an outdoor advertising tax they deem as an excise tax which is applied to ads on billboards, the sides of buildings and such. There are also taxes on rents or leases in some areas, so if you trade for a great ad or make a good deal to swap rent for your product or service, just know you might still have the obligation to pay the associated tax. Being aware of potential liabilities such as these will prevent you from running afoul of any taxing authorities.

Disclaimer

I am not a tax professional, any information or advice contained within this writing is for informational purposes and should not be relied upon when addressing your tax responsibilities. This information is meant to make you aware of some of the potential tax implications you may not have been previously aware of. ALWAYS check with an accounting professional for advice because every individual's tax liability is different, the tax codes are complex, often subject to interpretation and are ever changing. Please also be informed that any discussion relating to U.S. Federal and/or State tax responsibilities contained in this book is not intended or written to be used, and cannot be used, for the purpose of (i) preparing your taxes (ii) avoiding penalties under the Internal Revenue Code or (iii) promoting, marketing or recommending to another party any transaction or matter addressed herein.

EVERYTHING
IS NEGOTIABLE

CHAPTER 17

ADVANCED BARTERING

You can and should join more than one exchange if you have the ability to handle additional sales volume and have been making good use of the trade credits you are already accumulating. Belonging to several exchanges creates a larger network of members for you to interact with and you will be able to take advantage of the different strengths of multiple exchanges.

Items and categories that are typically challenging to barter, like travel arrangements, can become more readily available to you as you broaden your horizon by adding other sources to trade with. You can also comparison shop, as fees for the same or similar services may be different. As noted earlier, some exchanges have additional fees for concierge type services while others do not.

Reciprocal Exchanges

Exchanges can and do trade with other exchanges to make things available to their members that are not available within their own exchange or to supplement the needs of their members. This is a great way for an exchange to trade out of something they have an abundance of that their own members can't possibly consume within a specific time frame.

Examples of time sensitive items would be things like tickets for concerts, sporting events or Broadway tickets that will have no value if not sold by the time the event begins. These tickets can often be sold quickly, even within hours of an event, when one exchange emails availability to other exchanges in its network. E-tickets can be emailed or physical tickets can be picked up at a *will call* window by the purchaser regardless of how they paid for them, which further facilitates last minute transactions.

This allows box offices to hold unsold tickets as long as they can, trying to move them for cash, knowing they can unload them on the day of an event for face value, and sometimes for a premium in trade dollars through a barter exchange.

Reciprocal agreements expand options for trade exchanges to improve their member services while affording members an additional level of protection and representation. It's a win-win for sure if the need arises to settle a dispute.

Maximize the use of your cash by minimizing how much of it you spend in trade transactions. Purchasing nontaxable items that increase your *barter dollar to cash dollar* spending ratio is one way of doing this. Take advantage of all-inclusive vacation packages that include hotels. Some packages also include food and beverage, which eliminates all out of pocket expenses while you are relaxing on a resort's property. Also try to find all-inclusive packages which have transportation options included as well, this will turn a home run of a deal into a grand slam. Remember, a package offered as a vacation package could also be used as a business expense if you can conduct business or call upon customers in a resort area. Are you in the kind of business that can benefit from this sort of travel and write it off?

Buy Downs

Sometimes sellers require cash in a deal to make a transaction happen. If a deal is going to include some cash and some trade, I call it a *blended deal*. Negotiate down the amount of cash you are asked to put into blended deals so your cash percentage is reduced and do it every time you negotiate. Just because a vendor says they can't do a deal unless it's half cash and half trade doesn't mean that you can't negotiate this to sixty percent trade and forty percent cash or seventy/thirty in your favor. Remember, cash is always king in a negotiation, even more so in a barter situation. Any seasoned trader will usually still be highly motivated to make a deal to bring in some cash, even if it's considerably less than they initially ask for.

You can also do the reverse and buy down the cash portion of a purchase with additional barter credits to conserve cash.

Add a sweetener to the deal where you buy down the cash a seller is asking for by offering something to the effect of a dollar reduction for every two dollars in trade paid. Some sellers will go for this. I've seen people calculate a buy down for as much as five to one, meaning they paid a five hundred dollar trade premium to avoid a hundred dollar cash expense. The effectiveness of this tactic depends largely on your gross margins and the net cost of a bartered dollar to you.

The net effect of buying down cash dollars for more trade credits is very similar to the point I made earlier in the roof replacement deal about "overpaying" to complete a transaction. No matter how much you pay for a legitimate business expense, it is still tax deductible and therefore a benefit. The amount of this reduction could be substantial based on the tax bracket you find yourself in at the end of the year. This however is not usually a good reason in and of itself for conducting such transactions.

Sweeteners

The reverse of a buy down is adding some cash in an offer to sweeten a deal and result in larger savings of barter dollars that have greater value to you in other transactions. If you employ this tactic, you should be looking for a significant reduction in trade dollars for every cash dollar otherwise it will almost always be cost effective to pay the trade price. If you know your tipping point, then it should be easy to calculate where your limit should be in substituting cash for trade dollars or vice versa. As always, there are exceptions when this may work as evidenced in the T-shirt deal referenced in chapter eleven and you may use this tactic as a last resort instead of paying full retail for cash. The math will tell you if it pays.

Like / Kind Exchanges

Real estate transactions involving business or investment properties known as like/kind exchanges are swaps of similarly classified types of real estate that allow two property owners to create tax free transfers. See the appendix for a direct link to the IRS site that defines the rules for these transactions. Trade exchanges would be good sources for traders seeking to do a like/kind exchange if they are holding properties they would be willing to trade instead of selling as they will be introduced to others who are already familiar with the bartering concept.

Direct Trades

"Direct Trade"; two dirty words for trade exchanges because direct trades have no commission associated with them.

In a direct trade, the hurdles and barriers that intermediaries impose are removed. You are almost always dealing with the decision maker; it's just you and your trading partner at the bargaining table.

If you can sway a trading partner to accept your terms or acquiesce on theirs, then only you stand to gain. The challenge in direct trades, in addition to finding a suitable trading partner, is to balance the value in a transaction. Aside from the singular transaction types of bartering, direct trade works well between two businesses that can use each other's services on an ongoing basis. If a running balance is maintained with a trading partner, as long as the open balance waxes and wanes fairly or is acceptable to the party carrying the balance the relationship can work and may last for years. A simple example would be a marriage between a dry cleaner and anyone who wears business attire regularly that has services the dry cleaner would be interested in.

There's nothing wrong with making a commission free deal directly with a trading partner, and I would encourage you to do this as often as possible since conserving cash is the ultimate goal in bartering. However, if as a member of an exchange, you are introduced to another member of an exchange and complete a transaction, but circumvent using the exchange to process the deal in order to avoid being charged the fee that is due, then you have violated the fine print in the agreement you signed with the exchange for sure. The exchange will likely give you a stern warning on the first offense and expel you if you are found to violate this provision of the agreement again.

In this same vein, you should be careful not to *switch up* the exchange you process a transaction through if both buyer and seller are members in common of several exchanges, as this would be unfair to the referring exchange, which would rightfully feel they have earned a commission.

You can create as many of these types of relationships as you like. I find it interesting that some traders like to carry the balance, looking at it as money in the bank, while others prefer to owe it. I prefer to sell, then use services at my leisure, I just feel less obligated, as long as I'm comfortable that I will use the services I'm trading for in the foreseeable future. Either way, as long as a buyer and seller can come to acceptable terms the deal is a good one.

Three Way Trades

A trade exchange is the third wheel in a transaction acting as the middleman moving credits from one member to another so that members can make purchases from other members they do not sell to, or sell to members they don't buy from. Outside of exchanges, three way trades can be used to fill the void in direct trades when buyers and sellers don't have what the other wants to trade or the two traders needs do not align exactly.

Do you have a buyer that wants something you sell but you don't need what they sell? If you have a friend that could offer what the third party wants and you can trade something of value in exchange for your friend meeting that need, you could strike a three way deal.

Have a friend in your field? Why not swap inventory with another industry member to trade to the buyer for something you need? The circle is complete if A sells to B, B sells to C, C sells to A; all for equal value simultaneously. Obviously this is going to be more time consuming and fraught with additional challenges than a one on one trade, but there very well may come a time you find yourself initiating or being asked to participate in a three way trade.

Real Estate Improvements

If you own real estate, then anything you barter that is a capital improvement for the property will adjust the cost basis of your property and you will recoup these dollars tax free, if they haven't been depreciated, in the form of cash when you ultimately sell the property. If you are in the business of buying and managing properties as a real estate professional, then any barter transactions related to maintaining these properties will be tax deductible. You will also likely find as I did, that there are many ways to barter to reduce your carrying costs thereby further increasing the net income you already receive.

Timing

As the saying goes, *Timing is everything!* Every business has busy cycles, people in the construction trades often ebb and flow from being very busy to seeking new work. As we know, retailers are busiest around holidays and landscapers are busiest in the peak of summer. One key to successful trading is to use people in their off season for timely and less expensive work. In New York with winter approaching, landscapers need to keep their people busy when the season winds down, unlike in Los Angeles. But LA also has peaks and valleys in its business cycles, no pun intended; well maybe.

Whether it's certain times of the day, the week, or for seasonal reasons, avoiding the need to use services of members during their peak times will likely produce better results for you. In the landscape business for example, it is divided into two distinct segments of maintenance and construction. You may be able to barter maintenance year round but larger construction deals are generally more difficult in peak seasons. Most people would be believe it's related to the cost of materials, which can be a factor, but it's usually the opportunity cost of losing cash business that prevents these deals from happening. I typically get landscapers to provide estimates in their busy season and schedule significant work for the fall. This often helps a landscaper who is seeking new projects in the slow season to keep their key people employed rather than lay them off. In the fall, landscapers have also just come out of their money making season and are more likely to be flush with cash and willing to take on trade projects. The more flexible you are, the more successful you'll be when dealing with people subjected to timing limitations.

Residual Value

Purchases that have residual cash value such as cars, boats and real estate can be the best investments because they provide value while being used and can yield residual cash benefits when sold. Always keep an eye out for an opportunity to purchase something with your trade dollars that could be flipped later for cash.

I will confess I have never traded for a boat or car, which

typically only become available in used condition.

Fortunately, I have generated enough income to buy new cars and I already own a boat. If you have ever owned a boat, then you might know owning one boat can be one boat too many. That being said, I have seen many offerings for cars and boats which could be great opportunities for some traders. Trades that yield residual value are out there, don't rush to spend big money, but always be prepared for the right opportunity.

Deal Direct with Exchange Franchises

International exchanges like ITEX, that have offices in many states, are often franchises that have individual owners operating under the umbrella of a brand name. They also have a large office in Canada. Get to know the people in charge at as many exchanges as you can if you are actively looking for buyers. You might also speak to them about filling needs you've been unable to fill elsewhere. Create an email group so you can send out direct blasts when you have an offer or a need. Developing these relationships will only serve to expose you to additional opportunities.

Everything Is Negotiable

Bartering is as much about negotiating and deal making as it is about improving your bottom line.

You are in business to make money and every dollar you save, whether it's a trade dollar or a cash dollar, is simply several dollars less you have to sell to gain the same net/net effect on your bottom line based on your markup. If your markup is fifty percent, then you have to sell two dollars for every dollar you don't negotiate away from your costs or expenses in any deal.

Everything except the proverbial death and taxes, both of which we're always trying to challenge, is negotiable. Negotiation is truly an art, which can be perfected. Dismiss preconceived notions; the art of negotiating is forging a deal that two parties agree upon, nothing more and nothing less. When bartering, always apply the same rules of negotiating that you apply when spending cash, just be prepared for less flexibility from experienced traders on straight trade deals where the cash component is removed from the equation as an incentive to make a deal and occasionally you'll be pleasantly surprised by a deal you make.

The Strongest Person in a Negotiation

My first attorney taught me that the strongest person in a negotiation is the one that can walk away from a deal. Be that person. Especially when you are the buyer in a transaction, your ability to live without a deal gives you the upper hand. It doesn't mean you have to walk away, but it will allow you retain control of negotiations, ultimately achieving much better results than you started with. The fact that you can exercise this option whenever you choose is very comforting.

For small and simple transactions there usually is no need to negotiate, but as the stakes rise, remember your barter dollars are money and there is no need to leave extra money on the bargaining table; you want to make or save the most money you can, depending on which side of the table you are sitting at. When appropriate, ask for price allowances, volume discounts, negotiate additional cash charges or fees and use your buying power to your advantage. Be willing and prepared to accept "No" for an answer, it's not a bad thing. Also don't be insulted by buyers that make offers, it's just a negotiation tactic, if you don't want to be flexible simply decline any offer.

MONEY
SHOULD MAKE
MORE MONEY

CHAPTER 18

CONVERTING TRADE DOLLARS
INTO CASH

Yes, you can turn barter dollars back into cash dollars and improve real cash flow at the same time. Experienced traders are ALWAYS looking for opportunities to collect cash either in actual transactions or through peripheral activities.

While frowned upon by most trade exchanges, transactions that are part cash and part trade are sometimes a necessary evil. Blended trades, where cash and trade credits are used to make a purchase, facilitate deals that would never work otherwise. Large construction projects and other big ticket purchases often, but not always, fall into this category.

Jewelry Examples

As a jeweler I have lots of inventory which ages by default, that I need to move and would be happy to trade, without regard for the total amount of the sale. As an example, if you are like a newspaper publisher I did business with and have more than one hundred employees, many of whom are in management positions, you would have a healthy holiday gift list to address. So my phone rings with a request for forty pieces of jewelry ranging in price from two hundred dollars to a thousand dollars that I would be willing to trade to meet some of their needs. I put together a selection of items that meet this criterion and we set an appointment at my store to fill the request. The buyer selects items they believe are suitable for the people on the list from my offerings and we close a deal, typically for about fifteen thousand dollars. No cash, other than the sales tax, needs to exchange hands and this is a good trade for both of us. Everyone is happy, including the publishers staff.

The next time my phone rings, a customer I have bartered with before tells me he's in the market for a twenty fifth wedding anniversary gift and he is thinking he would love to barter a ring similar to one his wife saw at another jewelry store. The ring was priced at about nine thousand dollars. He thought maybe I could help him out.

Although grateful he thought of me, my response in this case is "Sorry but I can't offer you anything in that price range "full trade". I said this because I can't replace my higher end inventory easily without expending serious cash to do so. I would have had a significant out of pocket expense instead of him, to make the deal. I always avoid assuming a burden that will drain my cash flow to make a trade.

My customer responds with "I understand Bob, but if you would be willing to work with me, I'd rather buy the ring from you than the other jeweler since we've done business together before, even if I have to put up some of the cash or get something smaller." Now I'm listening. Obviously I could have tried to convert this to an all cash deal, and some people would, but we did have a relationship that I valued as well.

My response is "Tell me more?" By my calculations from the information provided, the cost to reproduce this ring is going to be about half of what the jeweler was asking, or forty five hundred dollars in materials, which still leaves a healthy profit margin; but I don't need to layout this kind of money to add barter credits to my account.

Numerous options start to run through my mind, the most appealing one being; ask for the forty five hundred in cash and barter the other forty five hundred making it a fifty/fifty deal for the customer at the same price rather than discounting for cash and incurring no hard costs beyond the labor to create the ring for me. This turns out to be fine with my customer who pays the forty five hundred dollars plus tax on the nine thousand dollar total price in cash and barters the remaining forty five hundred dollars of the price.

The customer received a cash dollar for trade dollar value on the forty five hundred and did not have to come up with the entire nine thousand dollars, conserving some of his actual cash. The traded portion also still reduced his actual cost based on his profit margins. I was able to receive trade dollars without incurring any hard cash costs because the cash sweetener covered my cash outlays. In this deal I created forty five hundred dollars in buying power with tremendous leverage to use later. A few deals a year like this should be reason enough to become a trader.

My customer was elated because he got the ring he really wanted for his wife and he continued to do business with me. He also referred several more cash customers to me, thanks in no small part to the beautiful ring that also became quite a conversation piece for his wife. This allowed me to reap a lot of rewards from those conversations.

The deal could have been made in a variety of ways. I could have absorbed some of the cash expense and bartered more if I was in that position, but it conflicts with the reason I barter which is to improve cash flow. This deal is a "home run" in my bartering world because on the flip side of the sale as a buyer I just put forty five hundred dollars into my account with no cost attached. This gives me tremendous leverage when I make purchases with these new found dollars. I literally have no cost because my trade dollars were all profit other than the exchange fees for the next forty five hundred dollars I spend. Can you say *free money*?

Referral Bonuses

If your exchange offers cash referral bonuses, take advantage. In addition to collecting money, you will create more opportunities to barter, have the first chance to conduct a transaction with the new members you bring in and make new relationships with local business people who will appreciate you opening the door to the world of barter for them.

Buy on Trade, Sell for Cash

Over time there will be opportunities to buy things on trade that you can actually sell for the same price or more in cash. Remember my box deal? I sold some of them on eBay for cash! I've also bought inventory such as Movado wristwatches on trade that I didn't have to expend cash on from a fellow jeweler who was looking to clear them out at deeply discounted prices. He was willing to accept barter dollars because he couldn't sell them in his store. Clearly he did not maximize his end of the transaction per my thought process. These types of opportunities leverage your cash because your cost of a barter dollar is not really the same as a cash dollar, but it was well worth it for me to take them off his hands and he was happy to see them go.

Keep in mind that a lot of people barter things they want to get rid of and they don't necessarily mark them up much, which will work to your advantage.

Understanding the true cash cost of acquiring your barter dollars as discussed in chapter ten will guide you towards making better deals. Using the Movado watches as an example, you can calculate how profitable it would be to buy them. For me, sometimes my cash cost to accumulate barter credits is fifty cents per dollar and sometimes it's free as in the case of the custom ring described above. Here's the math at a twenty cent cost per barter dollar to purchase the Movado watches I bought.

The wholesale cost of a nine hundred dollar Movado watch to a jeweler is four hundred and fifty dollars. The jeweler sold it at half off his retail or the same four hundred and fifty dollars it would cost me to buy wholesale. That is not to say this was his actual cost, but that's not relevant to me. My actual cash cost to buy the watch from a dealer would be:

$90.00 = Hard cash dollar cost
        (20% of the $450 selling price)
$45.00 = Exchange fee/commission
        (10% cash of $450 purchase)
$135.00 = TOTAL out of pocket cash cost
        Compared to the $450 wholesale

Wow, that's less than a third of what it would cost me for cash! This is the power of leverage in barter! Please note there was no sales tax added to the sale because I purchased the item for resale and therefore the sale is tax exempt.

I've learned how to accumulate barter dollars at an average cost of about twenty five cents on the dollar, which isn't bad in my industry, but not quite as good as people that have no hard costs because they barter their time instead of products.

Collection Agencies

Collection agencies barter their services and you can collect on old or bad debts without giving up a third or more of what is collected as a commission in cash. Hire an agency to improve your cash flow, they collect your money and it all comes back to you because they charge you their fee in trade dollars. Don't let people who owe you money cost you even more in the form of collection costs if you can barter those costs. Keep the cash and barter the fee. If the case escalates to court to acquire a judgment, you should be able to find an attorney willing to handle the case on trade.

Co-op Ads

Advertising in the generic sense should certainly improve your cash flow and put cash in your pocket, but a lesser known form of advertising using co-op ads will definitely generate some extra cash for you. Co-op, or cooperative advertising, is when vendors reimburse you or subsidize the cost of your advertising in return for ads featuring their products. The agreement may require the entire ad to feature their products along with the promotion of your business as a location for customers to make purchases or you might be required to designate a percentage of you ad space to feature the vendor's products. The amount of co-op money a vendor is offering has a lot to do with these details. Vendors that offer co-op ads will likely tie the amount of money they will give you to the amount of products you buy from them, usually calculated as a percentage of your purchases within a specific period of time, such as a calendar year.

The co-op agreement can be on a straight up dollar for dollar reimbursement for the full amount you are billed for ads you run featuring the vendor's products. The reimbursement can also be calculated as a percentage of matching funds, typically on a fifty/fifty basis where for every dollar you spend, the vendor will reimburse you for fifty percent of your cost, up to the credits you have in your co-op account.

If you pay for a co-op ad with your barter dollars and are reimbursed in cash you have created an immediate conversion of trade dollars into cash dollars in addition to reaping the benefits of the advertising. Ask your vendors if they have a co-op plan available.

**LOOK
BEFORE YOU LEAP...
THEN LEAP ANYWAY!**

CHAPTER 19

NOTES FOR BUYERS

Don't be afraid to buy with your barter dollars. BUY, BUY, BUY! You will find it is much easier to sell than it is to buy, so use every opportunity you get to spend your trade dollars. Replacing trade dollars will be easier than you think because your broker will send business to you. In all of the years that I have been trading, the one complaint I have never heard is that someone bought too much on trade.

Don't Overpay

This sounds straightforward but because of the leverage available using trade dollars, you can pay a premium when you barter relative to the cash value for something and still make a cost effective trade. Some people ask very high prices for what they barter because they are trying to leverage their buying power. By selling to people who undervalue their trade dollars and are willing to pay high premiums, these sellers gain an advantage over buyers.

Imagine getting two or three trade credits for a dollar and then spending them dollar for dollar in value at restaurants and other businesses. Now consider how the purchasing power of the same seller increases several times over if they are aggressive in selling and then resort to conservative tactics when buying, taking advantages of discounts and creating leverage in the opposite direction.

That's a healthy markup on the trade currency alone; producing what can be an incredible markup on the product or service sold. For this reason, the practice of overcharging is clearly frowned upon by most members and exchanges. Unfortunately exchanges do not police this as much as you might expect, with some being more vigilant than others, because higher value transactions translate to higher commissions, and these transactions do take place between willing buyers and sellers. Exchanges usually will not step in unless a complaint is registered.

In my experience, the victims of overpriced sellers tend to be those who have little or no cost attached to accumulating their trade dollars because they believe they have only given up their time to obtain them. I find this interesting because time is my singular most valuable asset and I would always want to maximize its value.

The valuation of my time doesn't diminish just because it could be represented as trade credits on a statement.

Don't overpay for goods and services, try to get at least a dollar for dollar value whenever you trade. That being said, you should know your real barter dollar cost as outlined in chapter eleven to make intelligent decisions. Remember in exchange transactions you are paying higher fees and your true net barter cost rises as well on overpriced transactions, so do the net/net math before paying too much.

This is always a personal decision, but I'd rather pass on a deal that is not value driven than expend extra trade dollars that will serve me better in another transaction. I choose not to overpay just because it's barter, as I have never considered my trade dollars to be *Monopoly Money*, even though I have heard others refer to it as such.

White Elephants

Don't buy white elephants! White elephants are big deals that let you spend a lot of your trade dollars, but you end up not using what you have purchased and sometimes worse; white elephants have carrying costs associated with them while you are not using them. Two great examples of white elephants that have carrying costs are time shares and land in the great open spaces of America. Time shares are abundant on trade because the sellers are offering empty space and down time in resorts and the like. Vacant land in undeveloped areas often has no chance of generating income or ever appreciating in your lifetime. Buying a piece of property hundreds or thousands of miles away from you that you may never find the time to step foot on is probably not a good investment.

Time shares can be good trades if you use them and the carrying costs are acceptable to you, but many people buy time shares with cash or with trade dollars because it sounds like a great idea at the time of the sales pitch. If the reality sets in that you aren't using it as you thought you might or the cash airfare to get to your destination is exorbitant you might come to the realization you've purchased a white elephant.

I understand many time shares today are far more flexible than they used to be and allow you to use other properties or time periods, usually with an associated fee. My point is don't be drawn into a purchase because it sounds too good to pass up, it must really meet your needs to be valuable. If you find it's not for you, get rid of it as soon as you can, but hopefully now you won't put yourself in the position of buying what turns out to be a white elephant.

"Want to buy some land?" There are many raw land deals and for the dreamer like myself. Buying up a few acres in the Southwest sounds like a great opportunity to build my own town, subdivide and sell houses and maybe even become my own town's Mayor. Before you get carried away, know these two things; the land I have researched is usually in remote places, sometimes with little or no access to utilities, so you would have to bring them in. Secondly there are taxes and usually cash fees to close these deals that can be considerable, so know all of the costs going in. If you are looking at undeveloped land that has a high probability of staying undeveloped for the next few generations, then move on, your trade dollars have better uses.

On the other hand if you can find a lot in a developed community without overbearing restrictions or carrying costs that aren't prohibitive you should seriously consider the value you might receive. If there is a chance for appreciation, then it could be an intelligent purchase. I have bought real estate on trade that I discussed in chapter four. It was a two family rental property that generated INCOME, that's why I bought it, avoid white elephants. Buy what you can realistically use. If you acquire a white elephant and buyers' remorse sets in, it is too late, so take extra time and do your homework before bartering for something that will cost you cash dollars long into the future, especially if it's not going to provide you with value you can justify.

You Can't Always Get What You Want

The Rolling Stones made a song with this title popular in 1969 and it applies in the world of barter. Have the tune in your head yet? Sorry.

Some things just are not available and "You can't always get what you want!"

There are companies and individuals that trade doesn't work for. If you need to take a Delta flight somewhere tomorrow, it's not likely that it will happen on trade. The notion that people are frustrated because they can't get what they want on trade has a lot to do with managing expectations. Be realistic and flexible, and accept that you can't always get what you want...on trade. This is ok; the overarching philosophy of bartering is to supplement your cash income within the limitations that exist in a non cash trading environment. It is equally unlikely that your cash income will ever be replaced with pure barter income, but it might be something to look forward to in your retirement years.

Can a Trade Exchange Go Bust?

Yes it can, it has happened before and it has happened to me, even though I did my research. It has been my experience that barter exchanges are sold or will merge with each other, but on rare occasions' they can just go belly up. I joined a small exchange, despite a real need to add another exchange to those I was already with, because I knew the owner and he had previous trading experience. Years later, the exchange became weaker and eventually closed without notice and I was left with a hanging balance. It seemed like a small disaster at the time but as I have found in most of my endeavors, what appears to be a disaster at one point in time often turns out to be less significant as time passes. I found two silver linings in that business failure.

First, I was able to write off the bad debt, reducing my cash taxes. Although I still lost some value, I recouped about forty percent of my loss in this manner. While the loss was still bitter to take, it was more palatable than losing everything. The stress of the loss was also mitigated by the lower actual cost to acquire those trade credits, so all in all I felt it was about a break even on the cash value side for me.

A year later I received a call from the owner of the very first exchange that my friend Mike encouraged me to join. It seems this fellow was getting back into the barter exchange business and he was looking for me to sign up. As you can imagine, building a business from the ground up, even with experience, is toughest in the first year. He needed new members, experienced traders he could count on to help him generate income and attract other members from the moment they signed up to kick start his new venture. He was also keenly aware of the fact the other local exchange had recently closed, creating an opportunity to fill a void that was created for some of the members.

At this point I had really significant balances with other exchanges and simply said "I'd love to, but no thanks". He courted me for a while; we discussed my situation and his. Eventually he came up with a deal too good to pass up and I found my second silver lining. In his infinite wisdom, this fellow offered to replace the trade dollars I had lost with the exchange that had closed down if I signed up with him and we ended up with a gentleman's agreement. His proposal was predicated on my selling products equal to or in excess of the balance he would credit me while spending those credits in relation to my sales. Meaning, I couldn't just spend down the credits and walk away. This would provide him with the benefit of having a jeweler committed to trading a significant amount of merchandise and services that he could use to sign up other members that would buy jewelry, thereby generating cash fees for his barter exchange. This would also balance his obligation to reimburse me for the lost credits over time and let me create new customers and sales.

I still do business with him, so we both have benefited significantly and continue to do so from the relationship, as he has earned years of commissions and I recouped the complete value of what was previously thought of as lost. As a bonus, a new trading connection was re-established that created many great opportunities for both of us.

Keep the Cash!

Don't sacrifice or substitute cash business for barter business. Barter works best when it supplements your cash business and should never replace it.

The goal is to free up disposable or discretionary spending dollars that maximize the value of your business assets and lead to more profits. If you are bartering items that cause you to tell cash customers you are now out of stock, then you are doing yourself a disservice. Always be on the lookout for chances to convert trade dollars back to cash or generate new cash using the myriad of ways you have now been exposed to here. Invent your own scenarios to barter in a manner that propels you and your business forward, incorporating new ideas within your existing business strategy.

WALK
BEFORE YOU RUN...
INTO TROUBLE!

CHAPTER 20

NOTES FOR SELLERS

Operating a cash business is challenging enough, when you start bartering there will be a small learning curve to overcome. There is nothing difficult about it, it's just different than what you're accustomed to. If you are a new seller, you should now be prepared when the sharks come out, so they won't take advantage of you. Here are a few general tips to help you navigate your way to better sales when you open your doors to barter customers.

Maintain Intelligent Balances

Don't allow your selling trade balances to get too high, moderation is the best advice here.

Unless you can afford to handle the carrying costs of large balances, which may include tax liabilities, it is prudent to balance the dollars you sell with the dollars you spend. The chapter titled *Taxes* explains this more fully.

Additionally, if you belong to a small exchange, there is always a chance that the exchange might not have enough members for you to effectively spend down the balance you have built up. Many members become frustrated when they develop large balances and then have trouble spending down; leaving them feeling their money is useless. This is more of a frame of mind than the whole truth and these problems are usually avoided if you do your homework when selecting an exchange.

Build Relationships

Build relationships, don't just sell. Strike up conversations that allow you to learn what your customer sells or the type of services they offer. Find out who your customer is bartering with effectively and what they are buying. Use this opportunity to recommend people you have had good dealings with and ask for recommendations too. Ask for non-member referrals to get cash business. You must ask; I usually do it the form of asking for a favor. I find it produces the best results. When you treat a customer right and ask properly, the customer will feel a sense of obligation to send someone your way to repay the courtesies you have extended them.

Set Limits

If you have a large inventory that you can afford to sell off or lots of free time, you may not feel the need to set limits on your offerings. However, your new found credits won't have any more value to you than stale inventory or lost time you expended to get them if you can't spend the credits for things of value to you. Setting sales limits in dollars or units of what you offer to exchange members is a good idea when you start, allowing you a chance to become familiar with the process. Unlike a missed opportunity to raise cash, acquiring trade credits is an easier process, your broker will manage the flow of business sent your way as you seek to increase or decrease your sales volume over time, so there should be no pressure to sell.

Many businesses supplement their inventory with items accepted on consignment from their suppliers like we do. Bartering items on consignment would create a negative cash flow that wouldn't be in your best interests so they should be off limits to trade unless the profit margins are so significant that you can justify assuming the cash expense of buying them to trade them.

Don't let buyers talk you into making deals that aren't in your best interests.

Know what your goals are and remember why you joined an exchange in the first place, to maximize your trading experience. You can limit your customers to dollars per visit or by dollars per month or quarter if it makes sense for your business model.

Don't Oversell

I could easily surpass my annual cash business in barter business but would not be able to effectively spend the trade dollars or replace the inventory I sold. For these reasons I often reach my selling limits and place my account on hold. Many sellers do not share this good fortune and always need to bring in more business. When I am trading, since I know I will eventually reach my trading limits, I'm careful to select items from my inventory that I see little to no immediate cash value in. I mean this in the sense that these items will be difficult to turn back into cash without discounting for a myriad of reasons.

Be Selective About What You Sell

Because we buy new inventory on a regular basis and cannot realistically sell everything we buy for cash, over time the remaining items grow old. These are the items in our inventory that we target each season to convert to trade dollars rather than letting them continue to grow even older. I can't tell you how many times I've looked at a ring that's been in my store for several years and said to myself I would buy it again if I sold it. There's nothing apparently wrong with it, but for some reason the ring would rather take up space in my showcase than go home with one of my customers.

After a while even the staff has a hard time showing an aging item because they would rather sell what's new. Before bartering we would have pieces in our stores that would age for five to seven years, tying up capital that could be put to better use. We now target these items to barter, thereby reducing our inventories average age without impacting our cash business or sustained profit margins.

Bartering is Usually Easier Selling

You will often find the task of *selling* is much simpler when bartering because you don't have to *sell* the customer. Barter customers are more willing to purchase than cash customers because there is a pent up demand to use their trade credits. Experienced traders want to take advantage of the leverage they have in their buying power when trading while others simply may not have extra cash on hand or disposable income so trading is also very advantageous to them. Therefore you should also experience significantly higher average sales per customer when trading. This will probably be a new dynamic in your sales transactions and should work to your advantage.

Money to spend seems to be burning a hole in some members' pockets, an effect not unlike the euphoria a kid experiences when set loose in a candy store. The kid just can't decide fast enough what to buy with their birthday money because they really want everything. Did you ever have that feeling? It might return again when you start trading.

The reason for the high demand and seemingly unlimited selling potential for me when bartering lies in the fact that I sell a luxury item with a relatively high cost ratio to retail and therefore a high perceived value. Members with balances in their accounts are always seeking "hard goods" for their trade dollars. Knowing there is always a large pool of potential business to draw upon is comforting and allows me to balance my trading in ways not everyone can. A broker can tell you if there will be a high demand for your products or service and it will determine how passive or aggressive you will have to be as a trader.

I know of members with the opposite challenge in the sense that they don't sell enough of their offerings and would like to expand their business because they have uses for more trade dollars. This can happen when there are too many members in a field within an exchange. Five bicycle repair shops may not find enough demand for their services in the same exchange. When this happens, these members often join several exchanges to meet their needs. Consider what goals you might want to achieve and limits you might want to set before you start bartering, and you will be a happier trader when you begin achieving them.

Save Money and Improve Margins

Sometimes there is a cost to liquidate, destroy or dispose of unwanted inventory so trade it instead. Don't dump that stuff in the corner of your warehouse; let a trade exchange find you a buyer. Items that appear to be obsolete or have no value in your market may have uses or be in demand in other markets.

Exchanges can connect you with markets that are geographically, culturally and fashionably diverse from your market.

Product Limits

You can select categories that will be off limits, which we do for watches as an example. We purchase name brand watches twice a year because the two primary selling seasons for us are May/June and December. Our vendors offer pricing discounts, financing or other incentive programs we like to take advantage of by placing larger orders. Therefore bartering several watches would reduce our selection between orders, potentially costing us a cash sale which would also further reduce our cash on hand by generating a need to re-order, resulting in a replacement expense. Watch vendors will also exchange models with us for newer stock, eliminating the need to mark them down or trade them. We would much rather convert other dormant categories of merchandise into trade dollars to unlock their value than trade watches we would need cash to replace, so we exclude watches from our barter offerings.

Gift Certificates

Selling gift certificates is an awesome way to bring new customers into your store, but they can backfire on you if you don't think through your objectives before issuing them for trade dollars. Gift certificates are going to be redeemed by the purchaser or someone they give them to and while not common, you might actually find instances where someone barters for gift certificates and sells them to a third party for cash at face value or a discount. The customers that buy or receive these certificates will certainly view them as cash so you must be prepared to accept them in the same way you would as if they were cash even though you sold them for trade credits. The goal in this section is to identify the advantages you would like to capitalize upon to improve your business and use gift certificates to accomplish it.

As an example, I noted we generally don't barter watches in our stores, but if I were to sell a large denomination gift certificate and a customer wanted to redeem it for one or more watches that could be problematic for me, defeating my intended purpose and thereby reducing the effectiveness of achieving my goals in trading.

If you have limits or restrictions for barter customers that you would want to apply to customers that will redeem the gift certificates you sell on trade, then they should be clearly stated on the certificates, if you do not want to accept them as a cash equivalent. The restrictions do not have to be the same restrictions that you place on gift certificates you sell for cash, but they may be. In my case where I do not want to trade watches, I could avoid this situation by simply noting "Watches are excluded" on a certificate and it would be fair; but it would also probably be perceived as quite odd to many customers receiving the certificates, unless the person who traded for them explained this to the recipient.

While we do not issue as many gift certificates as we used to, when doing so, we prefer to issue small dollar denomination gift certificates with no product limits. This accomplishes several things for us. The restriction we place on our bartered gift certificates states limit one per customer and that they cannot be combined for a purchase, this eliminates traders who buy ten certificates for one hundred dollars so they can buy the thousand dollar watch we do not want to trade. As experienced traders well know, this is the simplest way to circumvent that restriction. Because we are selective in higher ticket items we trade this works for us and we have other ways to sell the limited high value items we need to move out.

We view gift certificates we trade as a promotional tool to generate new customers rather than sell products. We focus on offering our services because these have lower costs, we have unlimited availability of labor that we are already paying for. We also have plenty of minor parts in stock that we can afford to trade, as compared to the high replacement costs of gold and Diamonds in our regular inventory. We want to create the opportunity for more people to visit our stores and become familiar with our merchandise and our staff. It's our staff's goal to convert these new visitors into repeat and long term relationship clients. We also generate some cash when recipients of certificates do make purchases for more than the face value of their certificates.

There is one thing to note about this system that works well for us. Since we have no real limits on most of our services such as appraisals, we can issue a gift certificate in any denomination limited to "Appraisal work" or for a specific service which we would trade as this eliminates our exposure to trading merchandise. We could also issue a gift certificate on trade in any manner that fits with the goals we have set within our business model. Think about your goals before issuing gift certificates that may adversely affect you.

Restaurants will normally barter gift certificates that are not good on weekends or holidays. They do this because it would result in the restaurant losing the opportunity to maximize their cash business in a very small window of time when they are typically booked solid. As you know, most restaurants have people waiting for tables on Friday and Saturday nights for hours sometimes, but these restaurants can accommodate you on a walk in basis almost any other time during the week. Certificates with restrictions allow restaurants to barter for new business during their slower periods.

It's also true that not every gift certificate you sell will be redeemed in a timely manner, if at all; thereby affording you some additional cash flow and potentially more profits. From an accounting perspective, you will probably be posting a liability on your books until the certificates are redeemed.

Train Staff to Free Up Your Time

I like to greet customers and have my staff work with customers; it's a style I developed that allows me to bring in many more customers than I could ever personally attend to properly. My staff is there to give Mr. or Mrs. Jones all of the time they need, often hours, because this is their primary

concern as a sales associate.

My goal as an owner is to keep finding new customers to keep my staff busy, their goal is to maximize every sale and encourage the customer to come back.

In order to provide better service to trade customers, I have

trained my managers and some experienced staff on how to

work with them. This allows each customer to interact with

someone representing my business that is well versed in my

policies regarding everything from our restrictions to our

policy for exchanges or returns. We like to make

appointments to control customer traffic on the sales floor,

manage our sales volume, explain any limits or restrictions up

front and provide an experience which hopefully exceeds the

experiences customers receive when they are spending cash

elsewhere. This is important because there is always the

chance these new customers may be spending cash with us in

the future or referring cash customers. There are no second

class citizens in my stores.

Having one or more staff members assigned to working with trade customers affords me the opportunity to schmooze with the customers or talk about their business while my staff is attending to their needs. This is one way you can learn a lot from others in a comfortable atmosphere that is conducive to frank conversations.

This is Not a Cash Transaction

Barter is NOT a cash transaction and should be conducted at your normal retail pricing. It is counterproductive to reduce your prices and accept trade dollars; this limits your leverage.

Reducing leverage affects your buying power and minimizes one of the great advantages to bartering your goods and services. The section "Understanding the Math" describes this in excruciatingly painful detail for those who hate math.

Collect the Cash

If you are required to collect sales tax, then collect it in cash; never include it for trade dollars. If you include the tax you will end up paying what should have been someone else's bill or worse; if you don't collect it and remit it to the tax man you could find yourself sitting with an auditor. You are also entitled to collect out of pocket expenses such as shipping or delivery and anything that has an out of pocket cost without markups that would traditionally be passed along to a consumer. Gratuities are always paid in cash. In the world of barter, the definition of cash is considered any form of money, not just the garden variety of green cash. Payment can be in the form of credit cards, company check, personal check or any other method you are willing to accept. We even have financing options. You just need to collect the money so you have it for the tax liabilities your sales create.

Making It Work

When cash is involved in a barter transaction it can become a deterrent that hinders closing a deal. Whether the cash due is an unexpected sum or not readily available to the buyer, the fact that they have found something they want to buy above their immediate means to pay for does not have to be an issue. We commonly use split tendered sales to *save* a sale.

Split tendered sales are those in which a combination of payment forms are added together to complete a transaction. We have done everything from converting the sale into a lay-a-way, to offering financing options, accepting multiple credit cards or combinations of credit cards and cash. We even accept checks and postdated checks depending on the potential risk. Be open minded and you will make more sales and more appreciative customers overall. An astute salesperson will know when to suggest ways to keep a deal together because the customer is trying to figure out how to raise the funds. We deal with this on a daily basis in the jewelry business. We call it helping customers afford what they want and we can be pretty creative, so you can be too.

Returns / Merchandise Exchanges

Think about how you would like to handle returns and merchandise exchanges. Is everything you offer on trade a final sale or will you take it back? If you offer refunds and a customer wants to return an item, then the solution is pretty straightforward. Merchandise exchanges can work a little differently if you have selling limits or restrictions that you would want to apply on an exchange in the same manner you did for the purchase. If you are dealing with a member that made a purchase and they were aware of any restrictions you imposed, then you would just follow the rules outlined for the original sale.

Using purchases made from my web site as an example, this would mean if the customer made a purchase from our barter web pages we would exchange the item for anything else on those web pages. This would exclude all of the same things that weren't offered at the time of the original sale. If a customer made a purchase in the store, then items off limits such as watches would be off limits on an exchange basis as well.

It becomes a little more challenging when someone gives an item they purchased as a gift to someone that is not familiar with the bartering concept and they wish to make an exchange, not knowing the item was purchased with restrictions. We handle this tactfully, offering exchange options or a refund to the purchaser if the recipient is not satisfied for any reason. The person wishing to make the exchange is not only now a customer, but is a cash customer that you should make every effort to satisfy.

Duty and Tariffs

Some businesses will have the ability to sell worldwide and clearly the internet facilitates this. If so, then be aware and beware of foreign transaction responsibilities which normally don't affect those selling intangibles such as hotel space, vacation packages etc. Shipping products that can be subject to duty or tariffs and have higher shipping costs in the exporting process may prove to be problematic if you are not familiar with the way to handle this.

For example, you should know that if you ship to Canada, your customer may have to pay duty based on the manner in which your product is categorized by the Canadian government to import the purchase. I've personally seen the Canadian duty range from six to twelve percent, which is based on where the item is going, the category declared and country of origin. Your customer may not be prepared or willing to pay the duty for your item and it can end up sitting in customs, where you may not be able to retrieve it easily, if at all. Duty can be more than fifty percent of the value of a product if a country desires to limit the import of an item for any reason you might imagine.

We had this happen to us when a trade customer in Canada refused to pay for an item because of the duty imposed by their government. Fortunately our exchange made the customer pay us for the item and left it up to them to decide if they wanted to claim it from customs or not. If you're selling something for cash and ship something to Canada C.O.D this can potentially be a huge problem as you may never get paid.

ALL
GOOD THINGS
MUST
COME TO AN END

CHAPTER 21

SUMMARY

Hopefully you have found some actionable intelligence within this writing. I've tried to present the concept of bartering in a manner that will motivate you long after you put this book down to change the way you think about your business and set you on the path that allows you to *Barter Your Way to GREATER Wealth*. As I have only shared a few examples of great trades I made within these pages, know that I have sold thousands of items and completed millions of dollars in trades that cannot be shared in this short space. Instead I've tried to pass along the concepts and some insight with respect to my thought processes, that took years to hone so you can have a head start and not have to experience the same learning curve that I did. If you benefit from this reading experience to any degree, then I have accomplished my goal.

Remember as you barter your way to greater wealth that you will also have opportunities to lift others with you and that wealth appears in many forms. Even though I only started my business with forty dollars, I have been wealthy for my entire life, long before I had money I had the things that people treasure most or seek to attain. The support and love from my family and the relationships I have made over the decades leave me wanting for nothing. I have traded for many of the trappings of success and enjoyed every minute along the way. The fact that I have been successful has allowed me to be much more philanthropic than I ever had thought I might be.

I hope sharing my experiences and perspective of bartering; might make you more successful and ignite or fan the flames of desire within you to improve your life and more importantly to me, the lives of others along the way.

I'd like to wish you a healthy journey along the path to greater wealth, which you should enjoy much more if you can employ some of these basic concepts to improve your lifestyle and the

bottom line of your business.

Respectfully,
Robert Borneman

This is a *Newsday* newspaper clipping from about 1995 or 1996 talking about barter after a major economic downturn. I was interviewed and that's me with a mustache in the photo! The mustache is gone but the basic principles of bartering have stuck with me for many years.

Jacks of the Trade

Businesses thrive using bartering system

By Collin Nash
STAFF WRITER

WITH THE ECONOMY in the tank, Robert Borneman's retail jewelry business was on the verge of going down in flames five years ago.

"It hit us hard," said Borneman, owner of two Diamond Jewelers outlets, in Centereach and Levittown. "With jewelry being a discretionary purchase, people were more concerned with buying staples."

So, Borneman listened intently when a longtime customer raved about bartering and how it could bring in more cash and more customers.

Now three years into it, Borneman has been able to trade much of his slow-moving inventory: Tennis bracelets studded with four-carat rocks. Gold necklaces and earrings. Baubles and bangles.

And he didn't have to drop his prices 50 percent to 50 percent as retailers normally do when they clear out inventory. Instead he bartered them without the steep discounts. As a result he racked up $90,000 in barter credits, most of which he used to place advertisements, something he hasn't been able to do in his 20 years of retailing.

Trading "has made all the difference in the world to us," he said.

Bartering has been around for eons. But a variety of economic changes, including the increasing number of self-employed people, have prompted more and more struggling mom-and-pop businesses to consider bartering to stretch their dollars.

According to the International Reciprocal Trade Association, an industry trade group, bartering transactions among small businesses jumped to $1.33 billion in 1995, from $707 million in 1990. Meanwhile,

the number of trade exchanges or clearing houses, which oversee the bartering transactions, climbed to 600 from 420, in the same period.

On Long Island, where small companies make up more than 90 percent of businesses, trading has made considerable inroads. National Commerce Exchange, one of the Island's oldest exchanges, reported that membership climbed to 2,200 this year from 875 in 1990.

"When the economy is good, trading is great," said Joyce Tash, president of the 16-year-old Jericho-based exchange. "When it's down, trading is better."

The exchanges act as bankers and record keepers for barterers. They credit members' accounts when they sell products or services and debit their ledgers when they purchase something. The increasing popularity of computers has made this process easier as barterers can pursue an electronic network to see what products and services are needed or available.

Advertising heads the list of the most bartered items. Also popular are restaurants, auto repair, printing and dental care.

Radio spawned modern bartering in the 1920s, when sales executives began trading advertising for hotel accommodations and other expenses. Then the Depression hit, and bartering all but dried up.

After World War II, the practice regained its prominence in the advertising community. That was the era when Los Angeles entrepreneur Marvin J. McConnell formed the Business Exchange International, the industry's first bartering clearing house. It exists to this day.

By the '70s dozens of exchanges were operating. They were given a boost in that decade by the personal computer. It was in this decade that the Financial Accounting Standards Board established tax and ac-

Robert Borneman at his Diamond Jewelers outlet in Levittown

counting guidelines for the industry.

Bartering got another shot in the arm in the 1990s as small businesses found their sales squeezed because of competition from aggressively expanding superstores. And the decade has also recorded massive U.S. layoffs as companies restructured in the face of global competition. Many laid-off workers, disenchanted with corporate life, became their own boss.

Between 1979 to 1994, the number of nonfarm entrepreneurs jumped 72 percent to more than 10 million people, the Small Business Administration reported in its 1996 State of Small Business report.

"Given the need among the self-employed for cash, particularly start-ups, bartering more and more is becoming an avenue for doing business," said Bennie Thayer, president and chief executive of the National Association for the Self-Employed, in Washington, D.C.

Just joining an exchange, however, doesn't guarantee that you can successfully barter your products.

"It's like joining a gym," said Tom Flood, vice president of Itex Corp., the Huntington Station barter affili-

ate of the Portland, Ore., parent company. "You have to work at it."

That means combing the bartering network and staying in touch with your broker at your exchange, Flood said.

It also takes longer to sell through the bartering system than more established channels.

Despite that, bartering remains an attractive alternative for many small-business owners.

For Donald Macina, who has run his own dental practice in Northport since 1987, bartering has been a boon.

A member of Barter Network Inc., which has a branch in Kings Park, Macina lauds bartering for the additional customers it brings him. "I've had clients come to me from as far away as the Hamptons and Cutchogue on the North Fork."

Bartering credits allowed him to take a vacation this past April with his wife, two kids and his father. They flew to Florida and boarded a cruise liner at Cape Canaveral, bound for the Bahamas. The trip cost $3,000 to $4,000, he said. His bartering credits covered all but a few hundred dollars.

Ken Mara often uses bartering to reward his workers. Mara, president of World Wide Security, a Garden City alarm and security-systems firm, last spring treated his top telemarketer and her husband to a romantic dinner for two and a Broadway show, complete with limo service. He paid the $1,000 tab with trade credits.

Mara had gotten the credits by installing and monitoring security systems for exchange members.

The distributor Clark Lift of New York Inc., based in Astoria, Queens, does a brisk business bartering its used forklifts through National Commerce Exchange, said Bill Landon, a sales executive who coordinates the transactions. The used forklifts sell for up to $35,000 each.

The company recently bartered for a $20,000 telephone system. And it spent $1,200 on promotional material without having to write a check.

Clark's biggest coup, Landon said, was to exchange equipment for a billboard announcement overlooking the Brooklyn Queens Expressway near the Williamsburg Bridge. "It's probably our most productive advertising location," he said.

Bartering also has its intensely practical side, as Borneman points out. For him, it's a godsend for the everyday things he needs. "It's the dry cleaning, the guy that fixes your car and the guy that fixes your teeth. Without it, I probably would have had to downsize."

APPENDIX

1. Recommended Trade Exchanges

a. National Exchanges
    i. ITEX Corporation (OTCQB: ITEX)
        http://www.itex.com
        ITEX Corporation
        3326 160th Ave SE
        Suite 100
        Bellevue, WA 98008-3418
        Main phone: 425.463.4000
        Fax: 425.463.4040

b. New York Exchanges
    ii. Tradeworks

        http://tradeworksny.com/
        Domenic A Casillo, President
        Tradeworks
        7B Main Street (Top Floor)
        Kings Park, NY 11754
        Tel: 631-269-4400 Ext. 102
        Fax: 631.269.4405
        Email: dcasillo@tradeworksny.com

iii.   NCE (National Commerce Exchange)

http://www.ncetrade.com
National Commerce Exchange
400 Jericho Turnpike, Suite 115
Jericho, NY 11753
Tel: 516-935-2280
Fax: 516-935-2316
24 hour authorizations: 516-470-6990
Email: info@ncetrade.com
Contact: Ken Paer

iv.   ITEX – New York Office
(ITEX Corporation (OTCQB: ITEX)
http:///www.itex.com
ITEX in New York
31 East 32nd Street
New York, NY 10016
Tel: 732-669-9300
Fax: 732-669-9310
Email: john.castoro@itex.net
Contact: John Castoro

2.   Craigslist Barter Link

https://www.craigslist.org/about/sites#US

Select a city, then the barter link under the "For Sale" section.

3.   Internal Revenue Service Links

a.   Barter Income - IRS:
http://www.irs.gov/taxtopics/tc420.html

b.   Like Kind Exchanges – IRS Rules:
http://www.irs.gov/uac/Like-Kind-Exchanges-Under-IRC-Code-Section-1031

c.   Sample Filing Form 1099-B – IRS:
http://www.irs.gov/pub/irs-pdf/f1099b.pdf

d.   Barter Exchanges Defined – IRS:
http://www.irs.gov/Businesses/Small-Businesses-&-Self-Employed/Barter-Exchanges

4.   Canadian Duty and Taxes Calculator

http://www.cbsa-asfc.gc.ca/travel-voyage/dte-acl/est-cal-eng.html

5.   Highly Recommended Accounting Firm
       (My Brothers Firm):
       Borneman & Associates CPA, P.C.
       Certified Public Accountants, Financial,
       Business & Tax Advisors
       40 Crossways Park Drive, Suite 106
       Woodbury, New York 11797
       Phone: 516-864-0770
       Fax: 516-864-0771

6.   Our Company: Diamond Jewelers

       www.DiamondJewelersOnline.com

7.   Contact the author:

     What would you be willing to trade for?

     Want to share a great trade you made?

     Interested in bartering a business consultation?

     Have any questions?

     Contact the author at:
     RobertBorneman7@gmail.com

www.ingramcontent.com/pod-product-compliance
Lightning Source LLC
Chambersburg PA
CBHW070222190526
45169CB00001B/50